D0007387

ASSESSING INTELLIGENCE

Intelligence tests are not perfect. They still measure *potential* inaccurately in the culturally deprived, or in those from cultures different from that in which the test was standardized, but they are *less* unfair than anything else. They are only a rough guide, but many experiments have shown that they are better than, and less biased than, unaided human judgment. They are better than guesswork, more efficient than trial and error, and they are improving all the time. They were invented as an instrument of social justice, a way of penetrating to the central capacity of a person despite his lack of education.

This book is written to amuse and instruct. I do not claim the tests within it will tell you *exactly* who and what you are. They are a good example of the kind of thing you will meet if ever you are seriously inclined to know yourself.

—Victor Serebriakoff

How Intelligent Are You?

THE UNIVERSAL
IQ TESTS

Victor Serebriakoff

BARNES
&NOBLE
BOOKS
NEW YORK

Copyright © 1968, 1998 by Victor Serebriakoff

This edition published by Barnes & Noble, Inc., by arrangement with Robinson Publishing

First published in the United States of America by Signet Books, 1968

All rights reserved. No part of this book may be used or reproduced in any manner whatsoever without the written permission of the Publisher.

1998 Barnes & Noble Books

ISBN 0-7607-1020-1

Printed and bound in the United States of America

98 99 00 01 M 9 8 7 6 5 4 3 2

FG

KNOW THYSELF

"Know thyself," said the sage—and this may be the most difficult piece of advice of all. Psychology, man's self-exploring discipline, is accepted as a science in the anglophone world; but in the francophone world it is still classed as a branch of philosophy. Philosophers of science agree that to learn its status as a science a subject must come down out of the blurred philosophical clouds to the earth of solidity, rigor and number.

If any branch of psychology has enough rigor to claim scientific status it is psychometrics, the science of mental measurement.

The pioneer work of Galton, Terman, Burt, Spearman, Binet, Guilford and Cattell has been consolidated and validated for half a century. There are few serious students of the subject who are prepared to reject the practical value of the mental measurement known as the intelligence test, however much argument there may be about their theoretical basis.

Big industry makes increasing use of them, the educationalist is frankly helpless without them, psychiatrists need them for a proper understanding of their patients, and faith in them and the demand for them by the general public is ever growing.

This is the layman's book, written by a layman for laymen. It is written to create interest in the subject, to give people a harmless opportunity to have fun by checking their intelligence and personality on tests which are parallel with and illustrative of scientific tests.

The problems and questions which are set have been prepared by an expert in intelligence-test setting. They have *not* been validated or subjected to the rigorous statistical tests which are necessary for a truly valid assessment. To use them is like measuring your height with a ruler that is only marked in feet: they are a rough guide, but better than nothing. If, when you have completed these tests, you doubt the results or want to know more, then you can have a test properly and more expensively supervised by a psychologist which will give you an in-depth answer.

Are These Tests Immoral?

Some people cannot square their egalitarian ideals with I.Q. tests. The very idea of trying to assess human talent and character is anathema—immoral, illegal, and fattening. Especially in the Communist world, the measurement of talent is ideologically unrespectable. In our own lands the innocence and perfectibility of unspoiled man is a quasi-religious doctrine. Marxists are at one with Freud in thinking that all important human differences are environmental, postnatal. Everyman's *rights* are equal, therefore every *man* should be equal.

Give me a newborn child, they say, and with the right treatment I will make him a genius. But they do specify a *human* child. They never ask for a monkey or dog or worm, so perhaps they may think there is *something* inborn. Even so, attempts were made in all seriousness to apply this doctrine by bringing up a chimpanzee side by side with human children. When they found that the monkey (after a period in the lead) fell behind in mental development they had to conclude that there may be some inherited difference. I expect we shall be told it was caused by choosing a mentally deficient monkey. The Marxists and liberal egalitarian environmentalists, it seems, are confusing the inheritance of wealth with biological inheritance.

Greatly daring, I suspect that if nature rather than nurture is responsible for the difference between men and apes, it might be partly responsible for the difference between the idiot and the genius, though I do not deny that the true human potential is often not fully realized.

A sensible view is that nature sets the ceiling and nurture decides how near to that ceiling we get.

But given the undeniable fact that human beings are unequal in achievement, even if not in potential, we still face the question: "Do we want to know?" Let me argue.

Why We Do Want to Know

In a primitive farming community where everybody toils for survival with simple tools, the advantage of being able to solve sophisticated problems may be little. But that is not how we have chosen to live in Europe and the developed world. The daily continuance of the immensely complex and interrelated commercial and industrial system upon which we depend for the thousand things and services we think we need each day, depends on putting a very large number of round and square human pegs into the proper holes. The continuance of our present civilization depends on finding occupants whose qualities fit closely to an enormous range of highly specified roles. "Home Heart Transplants," "Do-It-Yourself Brain Surgery," "Every Man His Own Industrial Manager," and "The Amateur Stevedore" are all equally inappropriate book titles. Our complex society works because we have found out how to put the right man or woman into the right job. The fact that we can do this so well is a sign that somewhere or other, seen or unseen, someone is making judgments about what a man can and what he cannot do and what his character is and how bright he is.

We start in the school. We sort and select (and we shall continue to). Despite the partial abandonment of streaming, and the preference for mixed-ability classes, despite Lehrer's satirical slogan: "Rank and position shall be awarded without respect to race, creed, class—or ability," we shall manage to sort people out and use them sensibly and comfortably in accordance with their powers and potentialities. It is safe to predict that all the attempts to abolish the classification of people as to ability will come to nothing. As fast as we throw such "discrimination" out of the door it will creep back in through the window.

At present we "discriminate" by using human judgment, by examinations, by degrees, and by qualifications—which means a lot of senseless "grinding" and education-free "coaching." But , as they become more perfect, we shall use more simple, easily administered, quick and efficient scientific tests, which are fair, objective, free from nepotism, religious or racial prejudice, influence and the old-boy network. They save time, money, unfairness, unhappiness, and mistakes. Above all, they are *predictive*.

But the tests are not perfect, they still measure *potential* inaccurately in the culturally deprived, or in those from cultures different from that on which the test was standardized, but they are *less* unfair than anything else. They are only a rough guide, but many experiments have shown that they are better than, and less biased than, unaided human judgment. They are better than guesswork, more efficient than trial and error, and they are improving all the time. They were invented as an instrument of social justice, a way of penetrating to the central capacity of a person despite his lack of education. They are attacked only by egalitarian down-levelers.

There is a great body of experimental evidence that establishes their general validity and very little which contradicts it (though much is made of it by the down-leveling procrusteans, of whom I shall have more to say later).

This book is written to amuse and instruct. I do not claim the tests within it will tell you *exactly* who and what you are. They are a good example of the kind of thing you will meet if ever you are seriously inclined to know yourself.

THE STORY OF INTELLIGENCE TESTS

Intelligence

The first human quality successfully measured was the most important, the one which divides men from the rest of the animal world and which is mankind's biological specialty—intelligence.

What is intelligence? One of the most frequent, obvious, and silly attacks upon intelligence is the dear old "How do you define it?" ploy. This is based on the Euclidian view that nothing is real that cannot be defined. As H. G. Wells pointed out, you can have fun abolishing many classes or concepts by defying people to define them. "Give me," he said, "any definition of a chair or 'chairishness' you please and I will undertake with the aid of a good carpenter to defeat it."

A horse, a clan, a face, happiness, pain, intelligence: we cannot define them so they don't exist, runs the argument.

But what *do* we mean by intelligence?

Lexicographer Johnson gave the word four senses. The first is commerce of information (mutual communication, distant or secret). The second is commerce of acquaintance (terms on which men live with one another). The third is spirit (unbodied mind). The fourth is nearest to the modern meaning: "understanding, skill." The modern sense of an *inborn* quality is altogether missing in Johnson's usage, which deals with acquired powers only.

Spenser shows a glimpse of the modern sense: "Heaps of huge words, unhoarded, hideously, they seem to be cheap praise of poetry; and thereby wanting due intelligence, have marred the face of goodly poesy."

Bacon's phrase could be read either way: "It is not only in order of nature for him to govern that is the more *intelligent* as Aristotle

9

would have it; but there is not less required for government, courage to protect, and above all, honesty."

Professor Sir Cyril Burt, the doyen of psychometricians, inspirer and president of Mensa, claims that the modern usage of the word "intelligence" derives from the science of psychometrics, not the other way around.

In France the pioneer of mental testing, Alfred Binet, used the definition, "*habileté*," which is fairly close to "ability." But Galton used "intelligence," and the word has come into a new use signifying the inborn problem-solving ability; Galton was the first clearly to establish this by his genetic studies.

The older meaning of the word, "information," has now almost disappeared and the Galton sense is the one usually intended. In other words the common usage derives from the new technical sense and not from the traditional sense of the word. There is, therefore, no legitimate complaint, because "intelligence is what intelligence tests measure." The circularity of this definition is really a feeble joke.

The definition of intelligence in an operational sense is relatively simple. It is demonstrable that the ability of human beings to perform specific tasks varies as between one human being and another. It is equally obvious that some people are good at some things and some are good at others. What is not so usually known but is equally true is that there is a relation, or rather a correlation (or *measured* relation), between skills and abilities. That is to say they are "unfairly" or unequally distributed. There is, alas, no law of compensation as there is popularly supposed to be which ensures that those who are good at one thing are poor at another and vice versa. On the contrary, the tendency is for those who are good at one thing to be good at many and those who are bad at one thing to be bad at many. Thus we get, *on the average*, a range from the versatile genius who can not only solve problems well but can paint and draw and think and write and even run and jump better than most, to the mentally subnormal who is below average at the majority of things.

Stop! I know what my beloved reader has started to say here. Wait! I deal with statistical generalizations and not with invariable laws. In the human sciences we are forced to deal with *tendencies*, not with invariable relations. It is pathetic how frequently otherwise well-educated people feel they have defeated a statement about a statistical tendency by giving one contrary example. "*You* say," they retort with scorn, "that children who are good at verbal understanding tend to be good at arithmetic—but I can prove you completely wrong; my Johnny is always top in English but he is useless at arithmetic. So there!" Useless to point out that one specially chosen case does not constitute a sample of great statistical reliability.

Let it be clear that this book lives in the real world of indeterminacy and adopts the simple biological strategy of "the best guess," leaving the unreal determinist world of invariable relations to the philosophers, logicians, and mathematicians who invented it and who still sustain it against all the evidence.

So my operational definition is simply this: "Intelligence is a factor which varies between individuals and is associated with the general level of ability displayed in performing a wide variety of different tasks."

Intelligence in this sense *is* measurable with reasonable accuracy, and it is a strong indication of the general ability or versatility of the subject. It is not simply a measure of your skill at intelligence tests, it is a measure of something definite and fundamental about you which affects and informs everything you do. Intelligence is not a virtue. Since it is largely genetic, it is nothing to be proud of. But it is not a fault either, and nothing to be ashamed of.

A Further Definition of Intelligence

At the risk of making confusion worse confounded I would like to add another to the many general definitions of intelligence. I prefer the simple operational one, but for the semanticists and lexicographers who are still obsessed with the idea that human concepts can be entrapped and held within the confines of a precise verbal definition I add the following.

Intelligence is a biological phenomenon. It is evident in any living thing or system however primitive. The universe is dispersing, breaking down, and moving from states of greater to lesser order by the ubiquitous increase of entropy; but it contains a number of self-ordering homeostatic entities which act as though they oppose the universal trend to move from order to disorder, from states of low to higher probability. In *this* class of entities there is a trend to build up order, to retain stability and to resist changes in form, to preserve low probability and even to lower it. This is the class of living things.

In order to resist the action of the change-forces in the universe these entities have to detect and counteract them. Since the process of counteraction often takes time these entities have also to be able to predict change-threatening forces, and to do this they have to have sense organs and receive information from the outside universe. They have to store it (in coded form) and transduce it into an appropriate output of instructions to their parts, organs and muscles so that they can resist the tendency of the universe to change their form beyond the level which they can correct. If the change passes beyond this level then a runaway change called death (or decay) sets in.

I define intelligence therefore as the capacity in an entity (living thing or artifact) to detect, encode, store, sort and process signals generated in the universe and transduce them into an optimal output pattern of instructions. The word "optimal" may cause some difficulty here because that is where "value" creeps in. I would define it as that which is best designed in the longest-term sense to ensure the preservation of the form of the entity concerned through time. It would include "evolutionary" changes in that form, i.e., those which tended to make the entity an even better homeostatic form-preserving device. It may be thought that my definition creates more difficulties than it solves, but there it is for what it is worth.

If we accept it, then the *measurement* of intelligence would be associated with a number of parameters of the described process. High intelligence would be associated with a large store of information, accuracy of coding, accessibility of information, long-term prediction, accuracy of probability estimates and ability to generate emergent or original behavioral solutions to problems. I will deal with this further in the part of the book devoted to creativity.

Testing General and Special Ability

The discovery that abilities correlate was crucial. It led to the notion that there is some general factor underlying the individual differences and contributing to a person's success in a number of skills. Thus Spearman accounted for *both* the individual variations of skill *and* the tendency for abilities to "cluster" in certain people. His "theory" is really a simple conceptual framework which helps us to think about human ability more clearly. Each person can be assessed for "g" (general-ability) and "s" (special-ability) factors. In any one particular skill your "g" rating contributes part and your "s" rating the rest of your score.

If you have high "g" and a high "s" for, say, music, then you will probably be a better musician than if you have the high "s" score with a low "g" score.

The only way to get at "g" is by using a number of different tests each of which is a *partial* test of "g." That is why we have batteries of different tests. Each type of test has a different "g" saturation or "loading," and the verbal ability has the highest "g" saturation. Most tests reflect this.

A well-designed intelligence test should not, of course, test the educational background of the subject. Even the verbal test items are usually chosen to avoid those that would be more likely to be known to a well-educated person. It is the ability of the subject to discern the exact shade of meaning of relatively common words which is measured, and not his knowledge of esoteric ones like "esoteric."

Are I.Q. Tests Reliable?

Strangely enough the idea of *measuring* reliability first arose from a consideration of the difficulties of intelligence testing. To what extent do test results repeat themselves? There is a test-retest variation and one of the methods used to sort out good tests from bad tests is to check it. An average deviation of 5 or 6 points is not unusual and the further from the average the score, the greater the variation is likely to be.

The Regression to the Mean

A little-understood phenomenon is the regression to the mean. Those around the average have an equal chance of being higher or lower when tested again, but those who get a very high score tend to get a lower one on retesting and those with a very low score a higher one. There is no mystery about this. In order to make tests administratively practical they have to be simple to mark. There should be a limited number of answers from which the subject must choose. They are closed-ended. When they are arranged in this style they can be marked by any clerk or even by a computer. If the questions are open-ended, i.e., when there are many possible valid answers and not all are listed, then only a highly trained specialist can decide between them; even then it is necessary for him to be of higher intelligence than those he tests. Now when we are using closed-ended tests with a limited number of answers it is possible for a well-trained monkey to get a score by going through and guessing at random. If there are five possible answers he would get one in five right on average. Therefore every test result is part luck and partly intelligence. They are so arranged that the luck element is small, but it is there. The probability of getting a high score is very low, but if we test a large number of people, as we do, then *someone* will win that particular sweepstake. So among any high-scoring group there will be a certain number who have had both luck and skill, and the higher the score the greater the chance that luck has contributed something toward it. Similarly, the lower the score the greater the chance that bad luck has contributed to it. On retesting, therefore, the frequency of a *repetition* of good luck or bad luck will (in a large sample) be low. Therefore the probability is that scores will tend back toward the average.

Culture Contamination

To what extent are intelligence tests fair to everybody? Measuring intelligence is an inferential process. We know of no way to probe the communication pathways of the brain and assess their general power to process information and transduce it into action. We have to base our conclusions on the behavior and treat the brain as a "black box," whose properties we can only learn by inference.

Matters are further confused by the fact that every individual goes through a different set of experiences from the moment of birth, and since the brain is the most efficient device known for sensing and being conditioned by external influences, what it *is* at any given moment is very much affected by what *has happened* to it up *until* that moment.

To get at the inborn (the genetic) qualities, we have to penetrate three layers. From the external behavior we can infer the internal mental efficiency, which is decided by a combination of the inherent qualities and external environmental experiences. From the second layer—mental efficiency—we have to deduce the third and deepest layer—inherent or inborn capacity. Professor Raymond Cattell distinguishes sharply between what he calls "fluid" and "crystallized" intelligence. The former corresponds to the inborn capacity, the potentiality, the ceiling which cannot be transcended. "Crystallized" intelligence corresponds to the measurable problem-solving abilities, the capacity to deal with information and produce appropriate behavior, or to make ticks in the right places on an I.Q. test.

Most psychologists believe that an intelligence test is only valid inside a given culture. Wherever you have a large number of children brought up speaking the same language and living in the same background of ideas and books and experiences, there is sufficient similarity in their environmental background that tests can be devised which can sort the children into classes which are associated with their genetic potential. But even the best tests, it is claimed, are culture contaminated; if we test people brought up in one cultural background—say, southern black children in America—by tests devised and standardized on those from another cultural background—say, American children as a whole—then we shall get a low reading from the former group. Of all the attacks upon intelligence tests this is the most valid.

By a corollary, intelligence tests cannot be used to gauge the relative intelligence of different ethnic or cultural groups. It is easy to standardize a test for each individual group and to find a mean and a standard deviation for that group. It is quite another to relate the

15

different means and standard deviations to each other. There is some dispute in the world of psychometrics about whether and how this problem can be overcome.

Some psychometricians like Cattell have produced "culture-free" tests which are claimed to be equally fair to those of all cultural groups, and there is considerable evidence that this may be so. Other psychometricists claim that these culture-free tests are weighted in favor of a certain type of intelligence and ignore other important aspects. The most difficult problem is that of the verbal ability. I pointed out earlier that most psychometricists agree that this has what they call the greatest "g" loading, that is, the highest association with the general ability factor which they are trying to measure. Unfortunately, it is this very ability which cannot be tested appropriately by "culture-free" tests since any language items must favor the language group of the language chosen. (It might be thought that language items can easily be translated, but the subtleties of semantic difference between different languages are such that a straightforward translation would be quite inappropriate.)

The Distribution of Intelligence

Like many other human qualities, intelligence is "normally" distributed. That is to say, if we put people into "intelligence" classes according to how bright they are, there will be a large number near the average. These will tail off in the typical Gaussian or bell curve, as people do for height or weight or any other variable human quality (see next page).

The Gaussian curve was derived from the theory of errors. It is the kind of curve produced by examining the variations of measurements of entities affected by a large number of random variables. It is the kind of curve that would be expected on a polygenic explanation of the heredity of intelligence. That is to say, it is the curve that would be produced if intelligence depended upon a number of genes and not just on one.

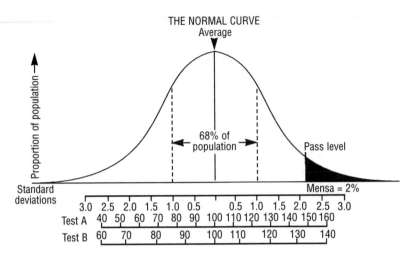

THE NORMAL CURVE
Average

Proportion of population →

68% of population

Pass level

Standard deviations

Mensa = 2%

3.0 2.5 2.0 1.5 1.0 0.5   0.5 1.0 1.5 2.0 2.5 3.0

Test A 40 50 60 70 80 90 100 110 120 130 140 150 160

Test B 60   70   80   90   100 110   120   130   140

A lot has been made of this normal distribution; perhaps too much, because a careful examination of the theoretical work which led to intelligence tests shows that the original experimenters started with the assumption of normal distribution and made this the test of their results' validity. The fact that they come out at the end with what they put in at the beginning is hardly surprising. Nonetheless, it is a fairly safe assumption and should be looked upon as a good working rule rather than an experimental conclusion. There would be a good case for saying, "Let us assume normal distribution until we have evidence to the contrary." Some evidence to the contrary is already visible at the lower end of the scale, as might be expected. With any complicated entity like a human being there are more things that can render it imperfect than there are things that can improve it. Evidence exists that there are two swellings to the curve at the low tail. One may represent birth damage; the other is as yet unexplained. The fact that this does not emerge from all intelligence-test data is due to the fact that cretins, idiots, and morons tend not to get into our original samples.

Taking the Gaussian curve to its logical conclusion, we would expect intelligence to extend infinitely in the upward direction. Also, at two standard deviations we get about 2%, at three, one in a thousand, and so on ad infinitum. But it seems unlikely to me that the curve would hold good for many standard deviations.

17

The Ceiling

A series of experiments with mice have shown that there appears to be a biological ceiling for the development of intelligence. Two groups of mice were bred apart as regards their ability to learn to run mazes; the quickest learners were bred together and so were the slowest. In a relatively small number of generations the two populations were so different that the slowest of the fast-learners group learned faster than the fastest of the slow learners. But further selection from the brightest of the bright produced *no* improvement, as it soon became evident that in a given stock of mice there was a natural limit to further development. My guess is that there is a similar ceiling to human intelligence. The analogy is a poker game. You shuffle your cards and everyone gets a hand; your particular hand is a matter of chance, and the probability of getting a royal flush is fairly low but it is predictable. By manipulating the pack and taking out some cards, you can increase the chances of a high hand but you cannot get anything higher than a royal flush—except by a miracle. There is a Russian story that the Apostles and Christ were playing cards: when the payoff came, Peter produced three queens, and Mark four kings and Paul put down a royal flush and turning to Christ said, "Now then, none of your bloody miracles." For our purpose we must read "miracle" as a new combination of mutations. The more complex a species gets the less likely an improving combination is. So we may have to wait some time for a bloody miracle. Meanwhile we could, if we wanted to, arrange that more people get high hands in the genetic poker game, or we could reduce the number of low hands. But that is a new and highly controversial subject which I will have the wisdom to leave at this point, otherwise someone will say "Hitler" or "eugenics" or some other swear word and all rational thought will cease.

SPEED

The Tester Tested

Another chestnut of the antitesters is the false paradox: "How does the tester deal with people more intelligent than he is?" The answer is a question of speed. The brighter you are the faster you solve problems, even simple ones. That is why nearly all intelligence tests are "speeded." That is to say, they are deliberately designed not to give the subject sufficient time. Many of those who complain because they cannot pass the Mensa tests say, "I didn't have enough time." Of course they didn't. Any test which gave *everyone* sufficient time would do a poor job of discrimination. However, there is some argument about this among psychometricians, and there are other types of tests called "power" tests in which what is tested is the ability to solve difficult problems: people are divided into categories according to their ability to solve them at all. It is much more difficult to devise this kind of test; they have to be much more carefully graded for difficulty and sorted into order of difficulty in the test. I agree from many years' experience in developing Mensa that there is something in this. But it may be difficult to produce a really convincing experiment to demonstrate the fact, if fact it is.

Dr. Furneaux of the Maudsley Institute holds a different view and has produced a theory of testing which is based purely on the time the subject takes to solve a large number of relatively simple items. This leads to the possibility of a mental testing machine, and some experiments in this have indeed been made.

Test Sophistication

Even though test times are chosen with particular care to avoid it, there is obviously a *practice* effect—the more tests you do the better you do them. In a properly validated test, however, the change in the score that can be made by practice is not great (about 5 or 6 points). It reaches a ceiling after a few trials and does not improve further.

Professor Eysenck has proposed that since so many people are getting intelligence-test practice it would be wise to absorb this cause of fluctuation by giving every child practice. The present book might be looked upon as a means to this end. On the other hand, the process of giving "training" in I.Q. tests is to be deplored if it takes time from real education. Also, children who achieve academic opportunities after such "training" might displace more promising ones who had not. This would obviously not be fair.

One of the most frequent questions to Mensa is whether it makes any difference to the result if the subject is unwell, has the flu, was drunk, tired, menstruating, or depressed when he or she took the test. The answer is that it does not make nearly as much difference as people think. Experiments show that temporary temperament is not a very big cause of variation. I hate to rob people of such a comfort when they do badly, so my advice is: wait till you have a headache, then take your test—it will give you a slightly conservative estimate, which is good for your ego if you *are* bright, and it will enable you to kid yourself that the results are not meaningful if you are not and cannot take it.

THE TESTS IN THIS BOOK

For each of the cognitive tests here, a preliminary test is given. This is to give you practice so that you do not come to the proper test without some idea of what you are about.

I recommend that sometime early on the day that you intend to do the test you should work through the preliminary test fairly quickly—but not so fast that you do it carelessly. Check your answers first before you go on to take the tests.

Timing the Main Test

I.Q. tests are designed to be administered under standardized conditions. A trained intelligence tester says exactly the same words in the same tone of voice in the same way and gives everyone the same timing. He also tries to preserve a cool, comfortable, and undistracting background, so that every batch of subjects has the same chance. He may have only variable success in achieving this.

The tests in this book are designed to take exactly 30 minutes and the answer will not mean much if you take more. If you take much less and the results are very good—well, I can pat you on the head, but I haven't worked out how much you should add to your score. It will certainly be higher than the book says. Timing yourself may be some distraction, so, if you are not too embarrassed, get someone to do it for you.

Peeking

Peeking, or having a preliminary glimpse at the main test questions before you do them, can be good or bad according to your objective. If the object of the exercise is to prove to yourself that you are bright, whether you are or not, then the more you peek the better. There is no harm in it because you are kidding no one but yourself. But if you really want to know, and are tough enough to take it, then peeking is out—it renders the rest of the exercise a complete waste of time.

Remember it is a speeded test so get as much done as you can. There is no penalty for wrong answers, and it is a good strategy to have a guess even if you don't know. Your guesses may be more guided by intelligence than you think. The obsessive checker is at a disadvantage; leave the checking till you've finished the last question. Don't rush too much. Work at the fastest speed at which you can put down well-considered answers. Don't get bogged down on one question—leave it and come back to it.

The questions are graded for difficulty, so most people will run into trouble somewhere through the list and find they cannot get much further. Don't worry about this—the test is designed to stop everyone somewhere.

Spend a little time over the instructions: you must understand them thoroughly or the thing is no go.

Each question earns one mark, so you can score 50 for each section of the cognitive tests. Now is the time to draw back if you don't want to be sorted or want to go on believing you are a genius. I cannot wish you luck because the more you have the more you will be deceived, and having said "Know thyself" I have to be consistent.

Those who proceed beyond this point want their brains tested . . .

VERBAL PRACTICE TEST

No time limit (18 questions). Try to practice working quickly. Answers follow Verbal Practice (VP) Question 18.

Analogies I

This is an analogy: *dark is to light as black is to white.*
Complete each following analogy by underlining two words from those in parentheses.
Example: high is to low as (*sky, earth*, tree, plant: sky is analogous to earth).
VP 1. dog is to puppy as (pig, cat, kitten).
VP 2. circle is to globe as (triangle, square, solid, cube).

Similarities

Underline the two words in each line *with the most similar meanings.*
Example: mat, linoleum, floor, *rug* (mat is similar to rug).
VP 3. large, all, big.
VP 4. empty, wide, entire, whole.

Comprehension

Read the following passage. The spaces may be filled from the list underneath. In each space write the letter of the *word which would best fill the space.* No word should be used more than once and some are not needed at all. The first letter is inserted as an example.

B

VP 5 & 6. Little (. . . .) of silvery mist (. . . .) to drift through the hollows while the light (. . . .) after sunset.

(A) eroded, (B) wisps, (C) before, (D) ended, (E) began, (F) faded.

Odd Out

In each group of words below underline the two words whose meanings *do not belong with the meanings of the other words.*

Example: robin, pigeon, *spade, fork,* eagle.

VP 7. man, cod, herring, boy, flounder.

VP 8. nose, mouth, smile, eyes, frown.

Links

Write in the parentheses one word which means the *same in one sense as the word on the left, and in another sense the same as the word on the right.* The number of stars in the parentheses corresponds to the numbers of letters missing.

il

Example: invoice (B**L) beak.

VP 9.   summit (T*P) spinning-toy.

VP 10. spot (**T) Dorothy.

Analogies II

Complete each analogy by writing one word in the parentheses *ending with the letter printed.*

eart

Example: high is to low as sky is to (. . . .H)

VP 11. young is to old as boy is to (. . . .N)

VP 12. airplane is to bird as submarine is to (. . . .H)

Opposites

In each line below underline the two words *which are most nearly opposite in meaning.*

Example: heavy, large, *light.*

VP 13. bold, bad, timid.

VP 14. tense, terse, serious, relaxed, provoked.

Mid-terms

In each row, three terms on the right should correspond to three terms on the left. Insert *the missing mid-term on the right.*

wo

Example: first (second) third : : one (T**) three

VP 15. mile (foot) inch : : ton (P****) ounce.

VP 16. triangle (square) pentagon : : three (F***) five.

Similar or Opposite

In each row below underline two words *which mean most nearly either the opposite or the same as each other.*

Examples: 1. *mat,* linoleum, *rug.*

2. *hate, love,* affection.

VP 17. reply, punish, repute, reward.

VP 18. disdain, feign, pretend, flatter.

ANSWERS TO VERBAL PRACTICE TEST

VP 1: cat, kitten. VP 2: square, cube (a circle is a flat shape produced from a globe, and a square is a flat shape produced from a cube). VP 3: large, big. VP 4: entire, whole. VP 5: E (began). VP 6: F (faded). VP 7: man, boy (human beings, not fish). VP 8: smile, frown (expressions, not features). VP 9: top. VP 10: dot. VP 11: man. VP 12: fish. VP 13: bold, timid. VP 14: tense, relaxed. VP 15: pound. VP 16: four. VP 17: punish, reward (opposites). VP 18: feign, pretend (synonyms).

VERBAL TEST A

Begin with exact timing. 50 questions in half an hour.
Answers on page 97.

Analogies I

There are four terms in analogies. The first is related to the second
in the same way that the third is related to the fourth.
Complete each following analogy by underlining two words from the
four in parentheses.
Example: high is to low as (*sky, earth,* tree, plant).
VA 1. sitter is to chair as (cup, saucer, plate, leg).
VA 2. needle is to thread as (cotton, sew, leader, follower).
VA 3. better is to worse as (rejoice, choice, bad, mourn).
VA 4. floor is to support as (window, glass, view, brick).
VA 5. veil is to curtain as (eyes, see, window, hear).

Similarities

Underline the two words in each line *with the most similar meanings.*
Example: mat, linoleum, floor, *rug.*
VA 6. divulge, divert, reveal, revert.
VA 7. blessing, bless, benediction, blessed.
VA 8. intelligence, speediness, currents, tidings.
VA 9. tale, novel, volume, story.
VA 10. incarcerate, punish, cane, chastise.

Comprehension

Read this incomplete passage. The spaces in the passage are to be filled by words from the list below. In each space write the letter of the *word which would most suitably fill the space*. No word should be used more than once and some are not needed at all.

VA 11 to 20. A successful author is (. . . .) in danger of the (. . . .) of his fame whether he continues or ceases to (. . . .). The regard of the (. . . .) is not to be maintained but by tribute, and the (. . . .) of past service to them will quickly languish (. . . .) some (. . . .) performance brings back to the rapidly (. . . .) minds of the masses the (. . . .) upon which the (. . . .) is based.

(A) neither, (B) fame, (C) diminution, (D) public, (E) remembrance, (F) equally, (G) new, (H) unless, (I) forgetful, (J) unreal, (K) merit, (L) write.

Odd Out

In each group of words below underline the two words whose meanings *do not belong with the others*.

Example: robin, pigeon, *spade, fork,* eagle.

VA 21. shark, sea lion, cod, whale, flounder.

VA 22. baize, paper, felt, cloth, tinfoil.

VA 23. sword, arrow, dagger, dart, club.

VA 24. microscope, telephone, microphone, telescope, telegraph.

VA 25. stench, fear, sound, warmth, love.

Links

Write in the parentheses one word which means the *same in one sense as the word on the left, and in another sense the same as the word on the right.*

il

Example: price list (B**L) beak.

VA 26. dash (D**T) missile.

VA 27. mold (F**M) class.

VA 28. squash (P***S) crowd.

VA 29. thin (F**E) good.

VA 30. ignite (F**E) shoot.

Opposites

In each line below underline the two words *which are most nearly opposite in meaning.*

Example: heavy, large, *light.*

VA 31. insult, deny, denigrate, firm, affirm.

VA 32. missed, veil, confuse, secret, expose.

VA 33. frank, overt, plain, simple, secretive.

VA 34. aggravate, surprise, enjoy, improve, like.

VA 35. antedate, primitive, primordial, primate, ultimate.

Mid-terms

In each line, three terms on the right should correspond with three terms on the left. Insert *the missing mid-term on the right.*

wo

Example: first (second) third : : one (T——–) three

VA 36. past (present) future : : was (I——–) will be.

VA 37. complete (incomplete) blank : : always (S——–) never.

VA 38. glut (scarcity) famine : : many (F——–) none.

VA 39. rushing (passing) enduring : : evanescent (T——–T) eternal.

VA 40. nascent (mature) senile : : green (R——–) decayed.

Similar or Opposite

In each line below underline two words *which mean most nearly either the opposite or the same as each other.*

Examples: (a) *mat,* linoleum, *rug,* (b) *hate,* affection, *love.*

VA 41. rapport, mercurial, happy, rapacious, phlegmatic.

VA 42. object, deter, demur, defer, oblate.

VA 43. tenacious, resolve, irresolute, solution, tenacity.

VA 44. real, renal, literally, similarly, veritably.

VA 45. topography, heap, prime, plateau, hole.

Analogies II

Complete each analogy by writing one word in the parentheses *ending with the letters printed.*

ear

Example: high is to low as sky is to (—— –TH).

VA 46. proud is to humble as generous is to (—— –H).

VA 47. brave is to fearless as daring is to (—— –ID).

VA 48. lend is to borrow as harmony is to (—— –D).

VA 49. rare is to common as remote is to (—— –NT).

VA 50. skull is to brain as shell is to (—— –K).

END OF TEST. 50 QUESTIONS IN HALF AN HOUR.
ANSWERS: p. 97.

VERBAL TEST B

Begin with exact timing. 50 questions in half an hour.
Answers on page 98.

Analogies I
There are four terms in analogies. The first is related to the second
term in the same way that the third is related to the fourth.
Complete each analogy by underlining two words from the four in
parentheses.
VB 1. mother is to girl as (man, father, male, boy).
VB 2. wall is to window as (glare, brick, face, eye).
VB 3. island is to water as (without, center, diagonal, perimeter).
VB 4. high is to deep as (sleep, cloud, float, coal).
VB 5. form is to content as (happiness, statue, marble, mold).

Similarities
Underline the two words in each line *with the most similar meaning.*
VB 6.   lump, wood, ray, beam.
VB 7.   collect, remember, concentrate, gather.
VB 8.   idle, lazy, impeded, indolent.
VB 9.   divert, arrange, move, amuse.
VB 10. antic, bucolic, drunk, rustic.

Comprehension
Read the following passage. The spaces are to be filled by words

from the list beneath. In each space write the letter of the *word which would fill the space most sensibly.* The words are to be used once only, and not all are needed.

VB 11 to 20. Reason informs us that (. . . .) of the gifts of (. . . .), including (. . . .) should lie (. . . .) and the voice of experience (. . . .) that if we allow the praise or blame of our (. . . .) to be the rule or (. . . .) of our (. . . .) we shall be (. . . .) by a boundless variety of irreconcilable (. . . .).

(A) sublimity, (B) distracted, (C) judgments, (D) none, (E) individual, (F) unused, (G) informs, (H) suggests, (I) motive, (J) heaven, (K) conduct, (L) peers.

Odd Out

In each group of words below underline the two words whose meanings *do not belong with the others.*

VB 21. knife, razor, scissors, needle, lance.

VB 22. bravery, disgust, faith, energy, fear.

VB 23. prosody, geology, philosophy, physiology, physics.

VB 24. glue, sieve, pickaxe, screw, string.

VB 25. receptionist, draftsman, psychiatrist, blacksmith, fitter.

Links

Write in the parentheses one word which means *the same in one sense as the word on the left and in another sense the same as the word on the right.*

VB 26. register (L**T) lean.

VB 27. hindrance (T**) link.

VB 28. contest (M***H) equal.

VB 29. blockage (J**) preserve.

VB 30. whip (L**H) tie.

Analogies II

Complete each analogy by writing one word in the parentheses *ending with the letters printed.*

VB 31. thermometer is to temperature as clock is to (————E).

VB 32. beyond is to without as between is to (————N).

VB 33. egg is to ovoid as Earth is to (————ID).

VB 34. potential is to actual as future is to (————T).

VB 35. competition is to cooperation as rival is to (————R).

Opposites

In each line below underline the two words *which are most nearly opposite in meaning.*

VB 36. short, length, shorten, extent, extend.

VB 37. intense, extensive, majority, extreme, diffuse.

VB 38. punish, vex, pinch, ignore, pacify.

VB 39. reply, tell, relate, disconnect, refute.

VB 40. intractable, insensate, tract, obedient, disorderly.

Mid-terms

In each line, three terms on the right should correspond to three terms on the left. Insert *the missing mid-term on the right.*

VB 41. beginning (middle) end : : head (W————) foot.

VB 42. precede (accompany) follow : : superior (P————) inferior.

VB 43. point (cube) line : : none (T————) one.

VB 44. range-finder (soldier) cannon : : probe (S————) lancet.

VB 45. face (body) legs : : nose (N————) knees.

Similar or Opposite

In each line below underline two words *which mean most nearly either the opposite or the same as each other.*

VB 46. liable, reliable, fluctuating, trustworthy, worthy.

VB 47. foreign, practical, germane, useless, apt.

VB 48. relegate, reimburse, legislate, promote, proceed.

VB 49. window, lucent, acrid, shining, shady.

VB 50. lucubrate, bribe, indecent, spiny, grind.

END OF TEST. CHECK YOUR WORK UNTIL TIME IS UP.
ANSWERS: p. 98.

PRACTICE NUMBER TEST

No time limit (26 questions). Practice working quickly.
Answers follow Practice Number (PN) Question 26.

Equations

In each of the following equations there is *one missing number,* which should be written into the parentheses.

PN 1. $21 - 6 = 3 \times (\ldots)$.

PN 2. $48 \div 2 = 20 + (\ldots)$.

PN 3. $4 \times .5 = .25 \times (\ldots)$.

cont.

Targets

In each set of missiles there are rules which allow the target number of the missile to be formed from the numbers in the tail and wings. In the example the rule is: *add the wing numbers and multiply by the tail numbers to get the target number.* Write the answer in the blank target.

Example:

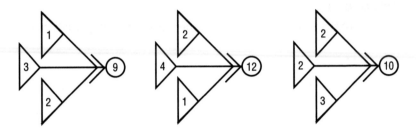

PN 4

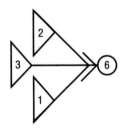 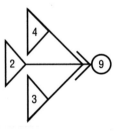 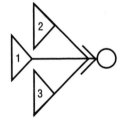

PN 5

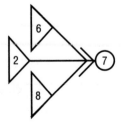 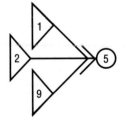 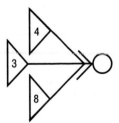

36

Series

Each row of numbers below forms a series. Write in the parentheses at the end of each line *the number which logically should follow the series.*

8

Example: 1, 2, 4, (. . . .).
PN 6. 2, 4, 6, 8, (. . . .).
PN 7. 18, 27, 36, (. . . .).
PN 8. 81, 64, 49, 36, (. . . .).

Double Rows

In each set of numbers below the same rules apply within each set to produce the numbers in the circles. Whether a number is in an upper or a lower row shows which rule applies to that number. In the example, the upper numbers in a set are added and then multiplied by the lower number to give the answer in the circle. Write *the correct number* in each blank circle.

Example:

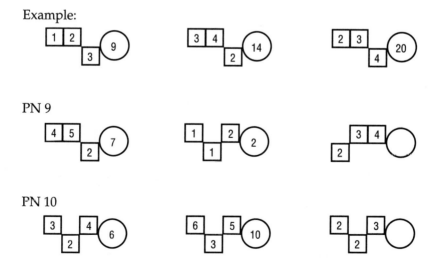

PN 9

PN 10

Mid-terms

In each line below the three numbers on the left are related in the same way as the three numbers should be on the right. Write *the missing middle number* on the right.

Example: 2 (6) 3 : : 3 (12) 4

PN 11. 11 (12) 13 : : 4 (   ) 6

PN 12. 4 (9) 5 : : 2 (   ) 3

PN 13. 25 (5) 5 : : 24 (   ) 4

Pies

In each diagram below the numbers run in pairs or series going around or across the diagram. Insert *the missing number* in the blank sector.

Example:

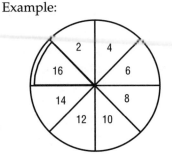

PN 14

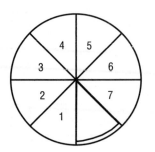

PN 15

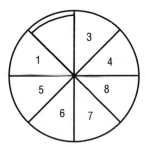

Matrices

In each square below the numbers run down and across following simple rules. In the example, the numbers in each row are formed by adding 1 to each previous number and the numbers in each column are formed by adding 2 to each previous number. Insert *the missing number* in the blank square.

Example:

1	2	3
3	4	5
5	6	7

PN 16

2	4	6
4	6	8
6	8	

PN 17

2	4	8
3	6	12
4	8	

Squares and Triangles

In each set of squares the numbers are related by particular rules to produce the number in the triangle. Each row has the same set of rules but the rules change from row to row. In the example, we add the numbers in the first two squares and subtract the number in the third square to give the number in the triangle. Write *the missing figure* into the blank triangle in each row.

Example:

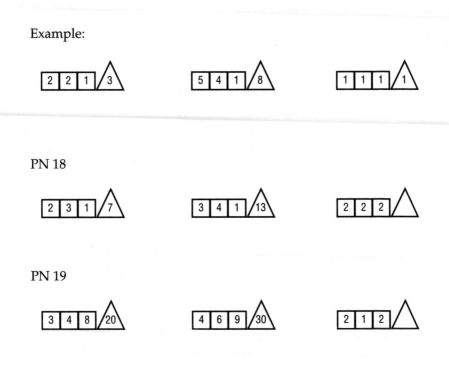

PN 18

PN 19

Rules and Shapes

The shapes tell us the rules of arithmetic applying to the number. In each set, the numbers enclosed by shapes are used *to produce the number not completely enclosed. Write in the missing number in each row.*

Example:

PN 20

PN 21

PN 22

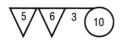   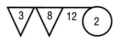   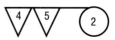

PN 23

41

Double Squares

The numbers in each row run in series. Write *the two numbers which should appear in the blanks on the right-hand double square*. In the example, the left-hand numbers increase by one at each step. The right-hand numbers are multiplied by two at each step.

Example:

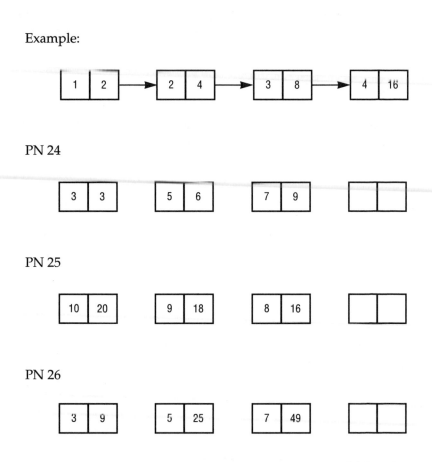

PN 24

PN 25

PN 26

ANSWERS TO PRACTICE NUMBER TEST

PN 1. 5. PN 2. 4. PN 3. 8. PN 4. 6 (Add numbers in wings and tail). PN 5. 4 (Add numbers in wings and divide the result by the number in the tail). PN 6. 10 (Add twos). PN 7. 45 (Add nines). PN 8. 25 (The numbers in the series are the squares of 9, 8, 7, 6, and the square of 5 is 25). PN 9. 5 (Add numbers in upper row and subtract number in lower). PN 10. 3 (Multiply numbers in upper row and divide by number in lower). PN 11. 5 (5 stands in the normal sequence of counting, between 4 and 6). PN 12. 5 (Add the outer numbers to give the inner). PN 13. 6 (Divide the left outer number by the right outer number). PN 14. 8 or 0 (Add one to each number successively in a clockwise direction). PN 15. 2 (Each pair of diagonally opposite numbers totals nine). PN 16. 10 (Both rows and columns progress by adding twos). PN 17. 16 (Rows progress by doubling. Columns progress by doubling not the original numbers but the numbers which are to be added to make the progression, i.e. add ones, add twos, add threes). PN 18. 6 (Multiply the first two numbers and add the third). PN 19. 3 (Multiply the first and third numbers and subtract the second). PN 20. 3 (Numbers enclosed within triangles to be added). PN 21. 9 (Numbers enclosed within reversed triangles to be multiplied). PN 22. 10 (Numbers enclosed within reversed triangles to be multiplied and product divided by numbers within circles). PN 23. 8 (Numbers within squares to be subtracted from numbers within triangles). PN 24. 9 and 12 (The first numbers in successive double squares form a series progressing by adding twos, and the second numbers similarly by adding threes). PN 25. 7 and 14 (The first numbers progress by subtracting ones, and the second by subtracting twos). PN 26. 9 and 81 (The first numbers in successive double squares form a series by adding twos and the second numbers are the squares of corresponding first numbers).

NUMBER TEST A

Begin with exact timing. 50 questions in half an hour.
Answers on pp. 99 and 100.

Equations

In each of the following equations there is *one missing number, which should be written into the parentheses.*

$$4$$

Example: $2 \times 12 = 6 \times (\ldots)$

NA 1. $8 \times 7 = 14 \times (\ldots)$

NA 2. $12 + 8 - 21 = 16 + (\ldots)$

NA 3. $0.0625 \times 8 = 0.25 \div (\ldots)$

NA 4. $0.21 \div 0.25 = 0.6 \times 0.7 \times (\ldots)$

NA 5. $256 \div 64 = 512 \times (\ldots)$

cont.

Targets

In each set of missiles there are rules which allow the target number of the missile to be formed from the numbers in the tail and wings. In the example the rule is: *add the wing numbers and multiply by the tail number to get the target number.* Write the answer in the blank target.

Example:

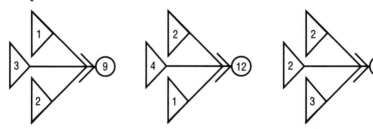

NA 6

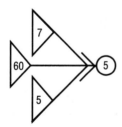 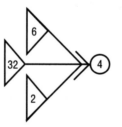 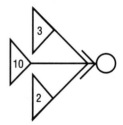

NA 7

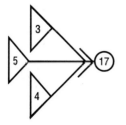 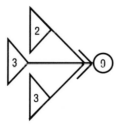 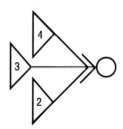

Series

Each row of numbers below forms a series. Write in the parentheses at the end of each line *the number which logically follows.*

$$8$$

Example: 1, 2, 4, (. . . .).

NA 8. 3, 6, 12, 24, (. . . .).

NA 9. 81, 54, 36, 24, (. . . .).

NA 10. 2, 3, 5, 9, 17, (. . . .).

NA 11. 7, 13, 19, 25, (. . . .).

NA 12. 9, 16, 25, 36, (. . . .).

Double Rows

In each set of numbers below the same rules apply within each set to produce the numbers in the circles. Whether a number is in an upper or a lower row shows which rule applies to that number. In the example *the upper numbers in a set are added and then multiplied by the lower number to give the answer in the circle.* Write the correct number in each blank circle.

Example:

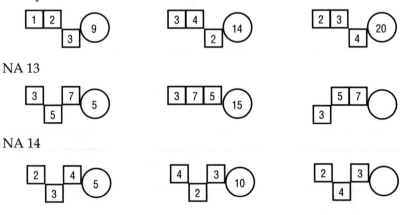

NA 13

NA 14

46

Mid-terms

In each line below the three numbers on the left are related in the same way as the three numbers should be on the right. Write *the missing middle number* on the right.

Example: 2 (6) 3 : : 3 (12) 4.

NA 15. 7 (12) 5 : : 8 (. . . .) 3.

NA 16. 3 (6) 2 : : 3 (. . . .) 3.

NA 17. 586 (121) 102 : : 653 (. . . .) 205.

NA 18. 444 (148) 296 : : 504 (. . . .) 168.

NA 19. 132 (808) 272 : : 215 (. . . .) 113.

Pies

In each diagram below the numbers run in pairs or series going across or around the diagram. Insert *the missing number* in the blank sector.

Example:

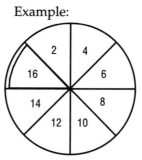

NA 20

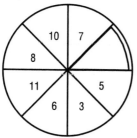

NA 21

47

Series II

Write in the parentheses *the number which belongs at that step in the series.*

NA 22. 53, 47, (. . . .), 35.
NA 23. 33, 26, (. . . .), 12.
NA 24. 243, 216, (. . . .), 162.
NA 25. 65, 33, (. . . .), 9.
NA 26. 3, 4, 6, (. . . .), 18.

Matrices

In each number square below the numbers run down and across following simple rules of arithmetic. Insert *the missing number* in the blank square.

Example:

1	2	3
3	4	5
5	6	7

NA 27

6	7	13
2	5	7
8	12	

NA 28

6	2	12
4	5	20
24	10	

48

Squares and Triangles

In each set of squares the numbers are related by particular rules to produce the number in the triangle. Each row has the same set of rules but the rules change from row to row. Write *the missing number* into each blank triangle.

Example:

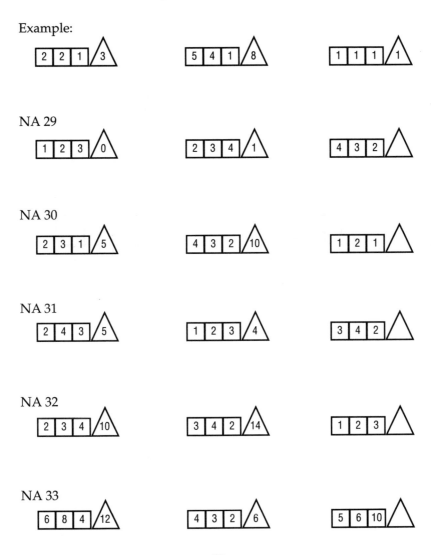

NA 29

NA 30

NA 31

NA 32

NA 33

Matrices II

Insert *the missing numbers* in the blank squares.

NA 34

1	2	2
2	3	6
2	6	

NA 35

4	2	2
2	2	1
2	1	

Rules and Shapes

The shapes tell us the rules of arithmetic applying to the number. In each set, *the numbers enclosed by shapes are used to produce the number not completely enclosed.*

Example:

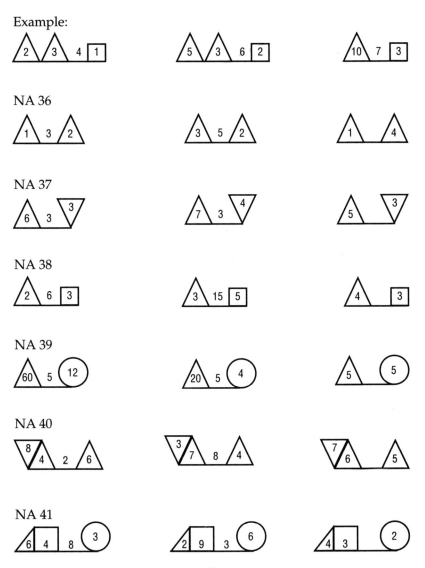

Pies II

Write *the missing number* into the space.

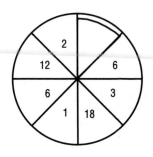

Double Squares

The numbers in each row run in series. Write *the two numbers which should appear in the blanks on the right-hand double square.* In the example the left-hand numbers increase by one at each step. The right-hand numbers are multiplied by two at each step.

Example:

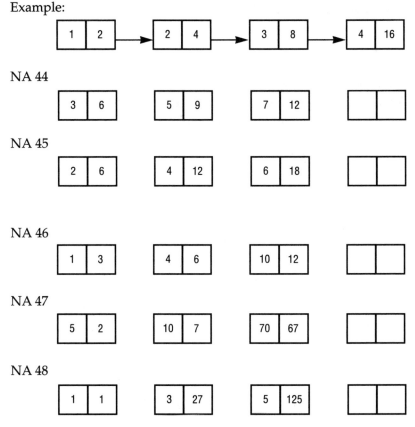

NA 44

NA 45

NA 46

NA 47

NA 48

NA 49. If $42 = A \times (A + 1)$, then A is (. . . .).

NA 50. If $162 \times 98 = B \times B$, then B is (. . . .).

END OF TEST. YOU MAY NOW CHECK YOUR WORK UNTIL THE TIME IS UP. ANSWERS: pp. 99 and 100.

NUMBER TEST B

Begin with exact timing. 50 questions in half an hour.
Answers on pp. 101 and 102.

Equations

In each of the following equations there is *one missing number* which should be written into the parentheses.

$$4$$

Example: $2 \times 12 = 6 \times (\ldots)$.

NB 1. $5 \times 9 = 15 \times (\ldots)$.

NB 2. $16 + 7 - 29 = 5 + (\ldots)$.

NB 3. $0.225 \times 4 = 0.75 \times (\ldots)$.

NB 4. $0.28 \div 0.35 = 0.5 \times 0.4 \times (\ldots)$.

NB 5. $81 + 27 = 243 \times (\ldots)$.

Targets

In each set of missiles there are rules which allow the target number of the missile to be formed from the numbers in the tail and wings. In the example the rule is: *add the wing numbers and multiply by the tail numbers to get the target number.* Write the answer in the blank target.

Example:

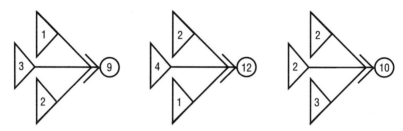

NB 6

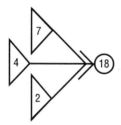 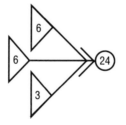 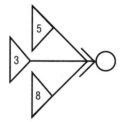

NB 7

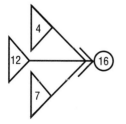 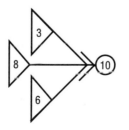 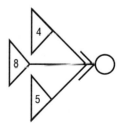

Series

Each row of numbers below forms a series. Write in the parentheses at the end of each line *the number which logically should follow the series*.

NB 8.   2, 6, 18, 54, (. . . .).

NB 9.   256, 192, 144, 108, (. . . .).

NB 10. 1, 3, 7, 15, (. . . .).

NB 11. 6, 13, 20, 27, (. . . .).

NB 12. 49, 64, 81, 100, (. . . .).

Double Rows

In each set of numbers below the same rules apply within each set to produce the numbers in the circles. Whether a number is in an upper or a lower row shows which rule applies to that number. In the example, *the upper numbers in a set are added and then multiplied by the lower number to give the answer in the circle*. Write the correct number in each blank circle.

Example:

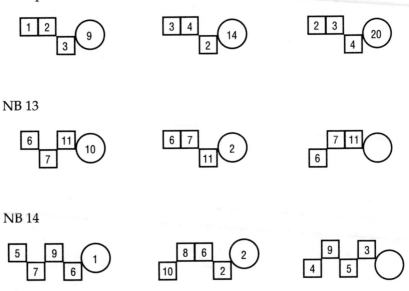

NB 13

NB 14

Mid-terms

In each line below the three numbers on the left are related in the same way as the three numbers should be on the right. Write *the missing middle number* on the right.

Example: 2 (6) 3 : : 3 (12) 4.

NB 15. 4 (11) 7 : : 8 (. . . .) 5.

NB 16. 3 (12) 4 : : 2 (. . . .) 5.

NB 17. 661 (122) 295 : : 514 (. . . .) 121.

NB 18. 205 (111) 239 : : 176 (. . . .) 124.

NB 19. 784 (112) 336 : : 968 (. . . .) 363.

Pies

In each diagram below the numbers run in pairs or series going across or around the diagram. Insert *the missing number* in the blank sector.

Example:

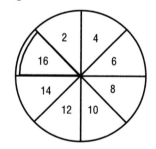

NB 20

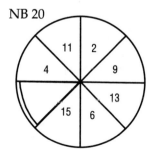

NB 21

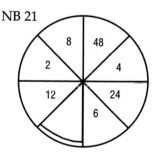

57

Series II

Each row of numbers forms a series. Write in the parentheses *the number which logically should be there.*

NB 22. 52, 45, (. . . .), 31.

NB 23. 43, 35, (. . . .), 19.

NB 24. 416, 390, (. . . .), 338.

NB 25. 92, 79, (. . . .), 53.

NB 26. 1, 5, 13, (. . . .), 61.

Matrices

In each number square below, the numbers run down and across following simple rules of arithmetic. Insert *the missing number* in the blank square.

Example:

1	2	3
3	4	5
5	6	7

NB 27

3	4	7
7	5	12
10	9	

NB 28

2	5	10
6	3	18
12	15	

Squares and Triangles

In each set of squares the numbers are related by particular rules to produce the number in the triangle. Each row has the same set of rules but the rules change from row to row. Write *the missing number* into each blank triangle.

Example:

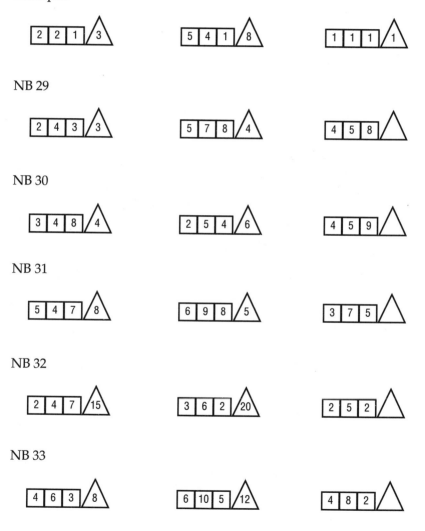

NB 29

NB 30

NB 31

NB 32

NB 33

Matrices II

Insert *the missing numbers* in the blank squares.

NB 34

3	11	8
4	9	5
5	12	

NB 35

9	4	3
18	3	9
12	4	

Rules and Shapes

The shapes tell us the rules of arithmetic applying to the number. In each set, *the numbers enclosed by shapes are used to produce the number not completely enclosed. Fill in the missing numbers.*

Example:

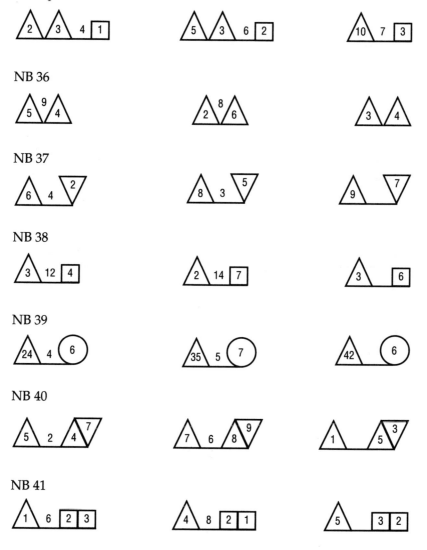

NB 36

NB 37

NB 38

NB 39

NB 40

NB 41

Pies II

Write *the missing number* into the space.

NB 42   NB 43

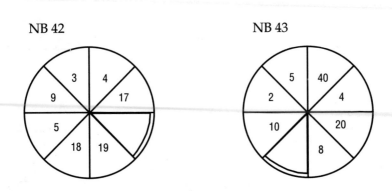

Double Squares

The numbers in each row run in series. Write the two numbers which should appear in the blanks on the right-hand double square. In the example, *the left-hand numbers increase by one at each step. The right-hand numbers are multiplied by two at each step.*

Example:

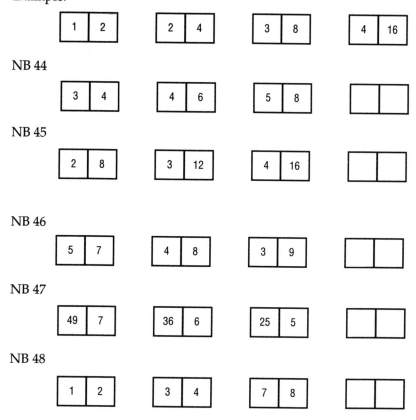

1	2

2	4

3	8

4	16

NB 44

3	4

4	6

5	8

NB 45

2	8

3	12

4	16

NB 46

5	7

4	8

3	9

NB 47

49	7

36	6

25	5

NB 48

1	2

3	4

7	8

NB 49. If $75 \times 48 = A \times A$, then A is (. . . .)

NB 50. If $84 \times 18 \times 49 = B \times B \times B$, then B is (. . . .)

END OF TEST. CHECK YOUR WORK UNTIL THE TIME IS UP.
ANSWERS: pp. 101 and 102.

PRACTICE SPATIAL TEST

There is no time limit, but work as quickly as you can. Answers follow Spatial Practice (SP) Question 17.

Turning

In each line below underline *the pair of shapes which, if turned around, could represent the same shape.*

Example:

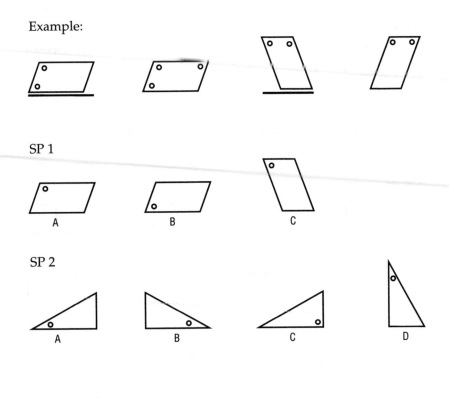

SP 1

SP 2

Reflected Forms

In each line below, two of the shapes represent mirror images of the same shape. *Underline that pair.*

Example:

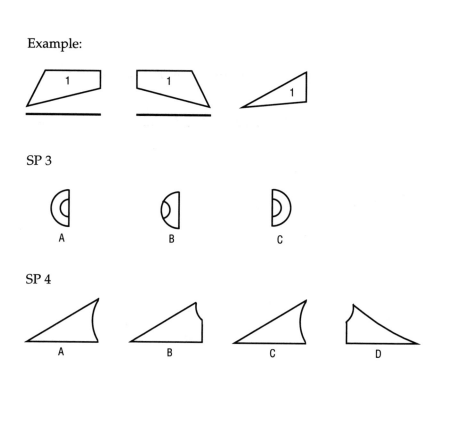

SP 3

A   B   C

SP 4

A   B   C   D

Reflecting and Turning

Imagine that all the shapes in this set are transparent sheets with a heavy black line along one edge and a dot in one corner. In each row, look first at the single shape on the left. If it were lifted off the paper, turned over, laid flat on the paper again and turned around "head to tail" it would resemble one of the lettered shapes on the right. Write in the circle at the end of each row *which letter shows the correct shape.*

Example:

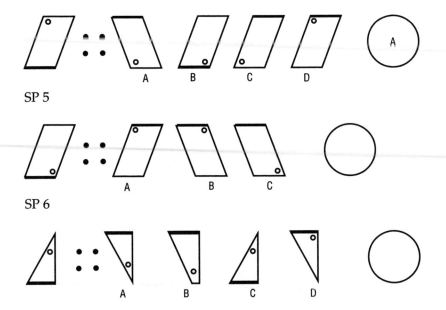

SP 5

SP 6

Potter's Wheel

In each row, two out of the three shapes on the left represent the same shape turned around—as on a potter's wheel, but not turned over. Underline *the two shapes on the right which are related versions of the pair on the left.*

Example:

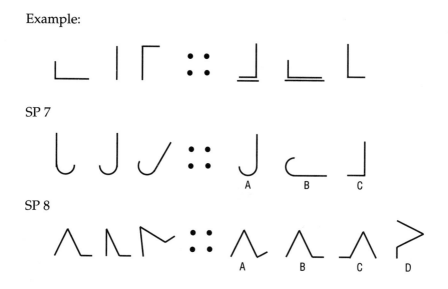

SP 7

SP 8

Fitting

The lettered shapes in the top row can be used to form the black shapes below. Write one letter, or more, in the parentheses to the right of each black shape *to show which lettered shape or shapes can be used to form the black shape.*

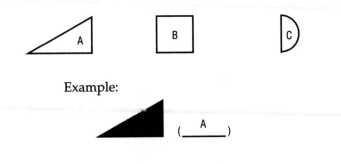

Example:

(___A___)

SP 9

SP 10

(_____)   (_____)

Following

The shapes on the left hand form a series. Which of the lettered shapes on the right continues the series? Write *the letter of the correct shape* in the circle.

Example:

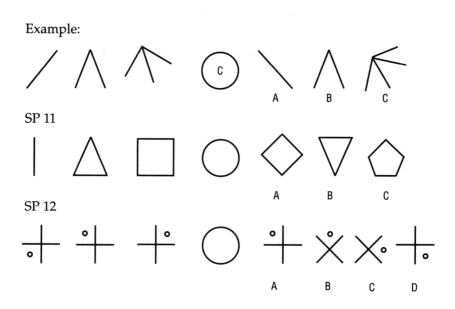

SP 11

SP 12

Counting

Each of these diagrams represents a pile of solid blocks that are all of the same size and shape. If any block is unsupported it is clearly shown as such. Some blocks are lettered. Write a number beside each letter in the column on the right to show how many blocks *touch* each lettered block. A whole face must touch. In the example, *blocks A and B are in contact with three blocks each: now start with SP. 13 and fill in the number of faces in contact with blocks A, B and C.*

Example:

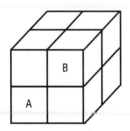

A	3
B	3

SP 13

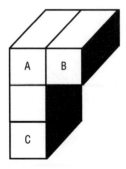

A	
B	
B	

Visualizing

Designs were drawn on some faces of these cubes. No design appears on the face of more than one cube. There are two blank faces on each cube. In each row some of the drawings are the same cube turned around. If a cube *can* be the same as another, assume it *is* the same. Write in the circle at the end of each row *the least number of different cubes represented in the row*. In the example, the second and third drawings are the same cube turned around.

Example:

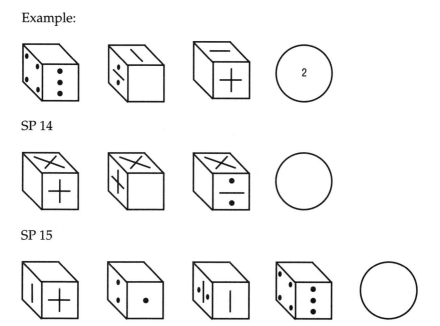

SP 14

SP 15

Analogies

In each row the first shape is related to the second shape in the same way that the third shape is related to the fourth. Underline *the shape on the right which should be the fourth shape.*

Example:

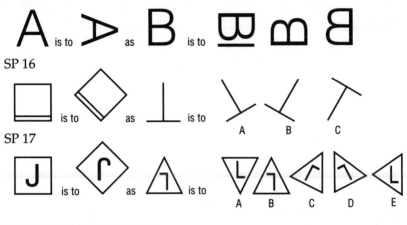

SP 16

SP 17

END OF PRACTICE TEST.

ANSWERS TO PRACTICE SPATIAL TEST

SP 1. B, C. SP 2. A, D. SP 3. A, C. SP 4. B, D. SP 5. B. SP 6. A. SP 7. A, B. SP 8. B, D. SP 9. A. SP 10. A, B, C. SP 11. C (a line has two points, a triangle three, a square four, and a pentagon five). SP 12. D (the dot moves in a clockwise direction around successive quadrants). SP 13. A2, B1, C1. SP 14. 1. SP 15. 2 (the first and third drawings represent one cube and the second and fourth drawings represent another cube). SP 16. B (the shapes are tilted to the right at an angle of 45°). SP 17. E (the outlines of the second and fourth shapes are tilted at 45° and the inner shapes are turned upside down).

72

SPATIAL TEST A

Begin with exact timing. 50 questions in half an hour.
Answers on p. 103.

see over:

Turning

On each line below, underline *the pair of shapes which, if turned around, could represent the same one.*

Example:

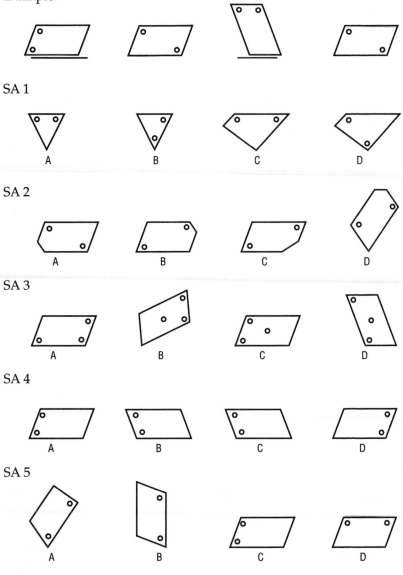

SA 1

SA 2

SA 3

SA 4

SA 5

Reflected Forms

In each of these lines, two of the shapes represent mirror images of the same shape. *Underline that pair.*

Example:

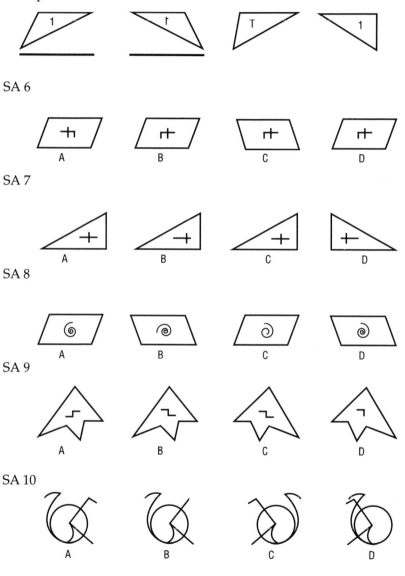

SA 6

SA 7

SA 8

SA 9

SA 10

Reflecting and Turning

Imagine that all the shapes in this set are transparent sheets with a heavy black line along one edge and a dot in one corner. One of the right-hand set of shapes represents the left-hand one, turned over like a pancake and then turned upside down. *Write its letter in the blank circle.*

Example:

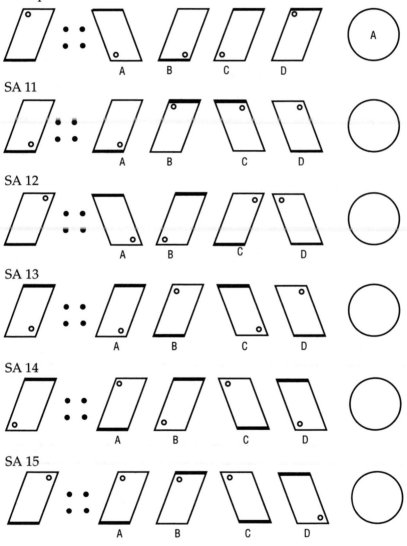

SA 11

SA 12

SA 13

SA 14

SA 15

Potter's Wheel

In each row, two of the three shapes on the left represent the same shape turned around but not over. Underline *two of the shapes which are rotated versions of the pair on the left*.

Example:

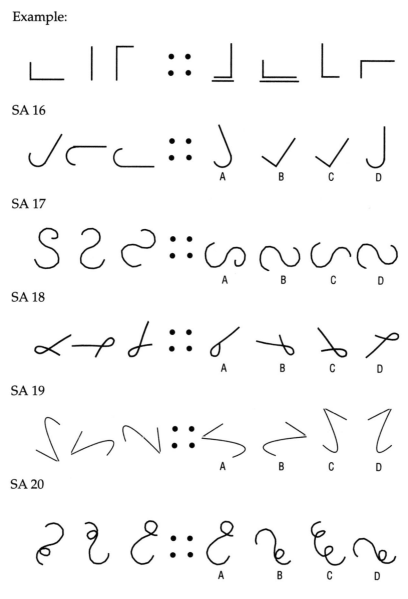

SA 16

SA 17

SA 18

SA 19

SA 20

Fitting

The lettered shapes in the top row can be used to form the black shapes below. Write one letter, or more, in the parentheses below each black shape to show *which lettered shape, or shapes, can be used to form the black shape.*

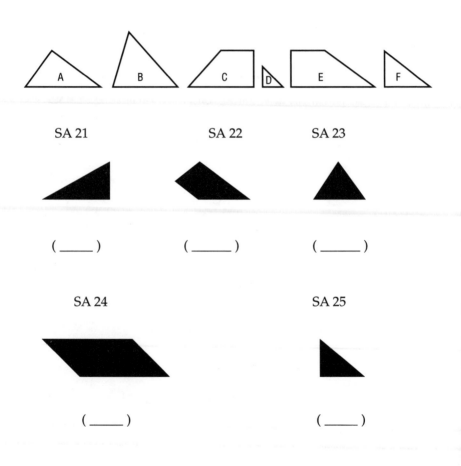

SA 21

SA 22

SA 23

(____)

(____)

(____)

SA 24

SA 25

(____)

(____)

Following

The shapes on the left form a series. *Which of the letters of the shapes on the right continues the series?* Write the letter of the correct shape in the circle.

Example:

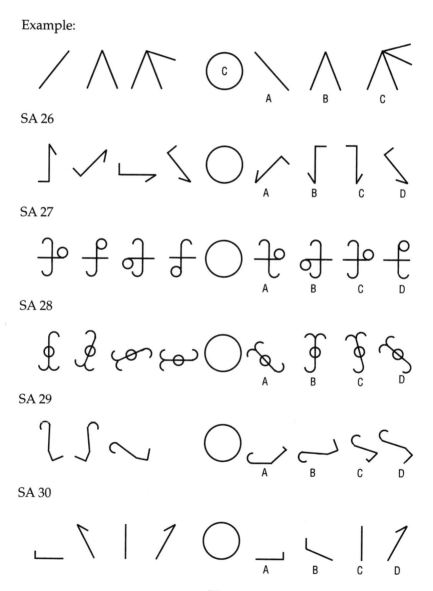

SA 26

SA 27

SA 28

SA 29

SA 30

Counting

The piles of blocks shown are solid. Any block without support is shown as such. Each diagram represents a pile of exactly similar blocks. Write a number beside each letter in the column *to show how many other blocks touch the block indicated by each letter.* A face, not just an edge, must touch. The first letters have been matched with numbers as an example, showing that block A touches three other blocks.

SA 31

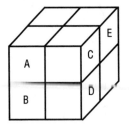

A	3	D	
B	3	E	
C			

SA 32

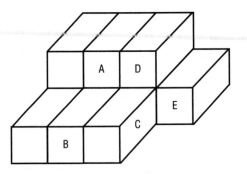

A		D	
B		E	
C			

SA 33

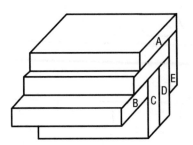

A		D	
B		E	
C			

80

SA 34

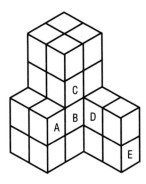

A		D	
B		E	
C			

SA 35

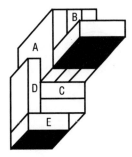

A		D	
B		E	
C			

Visualizing

Designs were drawn on some faces of these cubes. No design appears on the face of more than one cube. There are two blank faces on each cube. In each row some of the drawings are the same cube turned around. If a cube *can* be the same as another, assume it *is* the same. Write in the circle at the end of each row *the least number of different cubes represented in the row.* In the example, the second and third drawings are the same cube turned around.

Example:

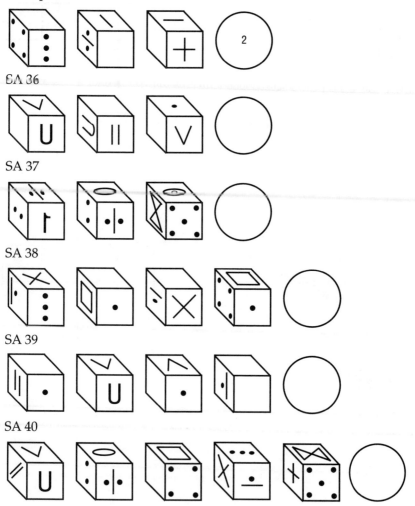

SA 36

SA 37

SA 38

SA 39

SA 40

Analogies

In each row, the first shape is related to the second shape in the same way that the third shape is related to the fourth. Underline *the figure on the right which should be the fourth shape.*

Example:

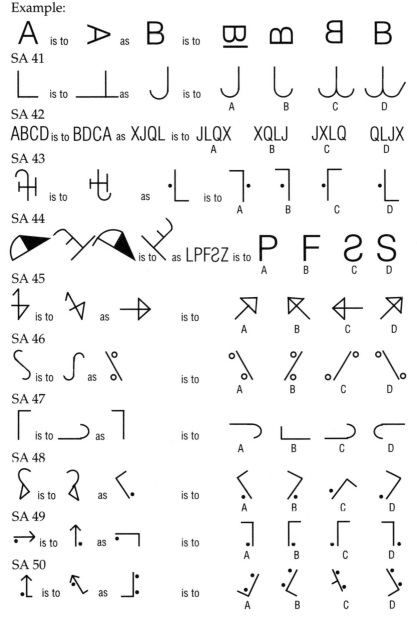

SA 41

SA 42

SA 43

SA 44

SA 45

SA 46

SA 47

SA 48

SA 49

SA 50

END OF TEST. CHECK YOUR WORK UNTIL TIME IS UP.
ANSWERS: p. 103.

SPATIAL TEST B

Begin with exact timing. 50 questions in half an hour. Answers on page 104.

see over:

Turning

On each line below, underline *the pair of shapes which, if turned around, could represent the same one.*

Example:

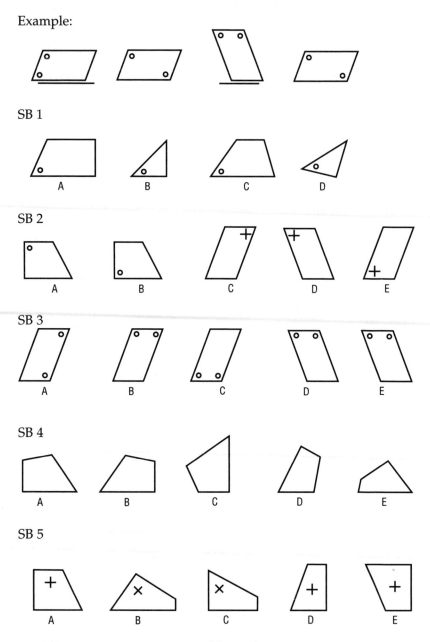

SB 1

A B C D

SB 2

A B C D E

SB 3

A B C D E

SB 4

A B C D E

SB 5

A B C D E

Reflected Forms

On each of these lines, two of the shapes represent mirror images of the same shape. *Underline that pair.*

Example:

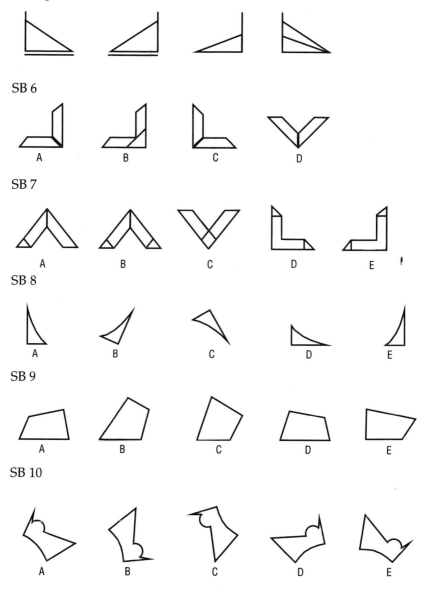

SB 6

A   B   C   D

SB 7

A   B   C   D   E

SB 8

A   B   C   D   E

SB 9

A   B   C   D   E

SB 10

A   B   C   D   E

Reflecting and Turning

Imagine that all the shapes in this set are transparent sheets with a heavy black line along one edge and a dot in one corner. One of the right-hand set of shapes represents the left-hand one, turned over like a pancake and then turned upside down. *Write its letter in the blank circle.*

Example:

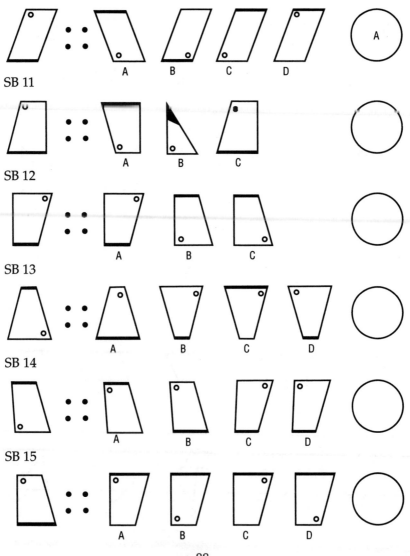

SB 11

SB 12

SB 13

SB 14

SB 15

88

Potter's Wheel

In each row, two of the three shapes on the left represent the same shape turned around but not over. Underline *two of the shapes which are rotated versions of the pair on the left.*

Example:

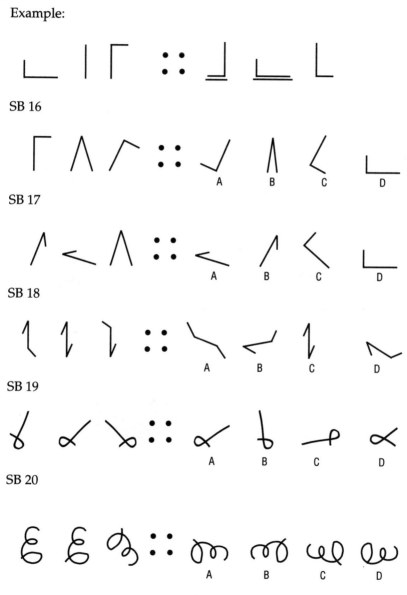

SB 16

SB 17

SB 18

SB 19

SB 20

Fitting

The lettered shapes in the top row can be used to form the black numbered shapes below. Write one letter, or more, in the parentheses below each black shape *to show which lettered shape, or shapes, can be used to make the shape.*

Example:

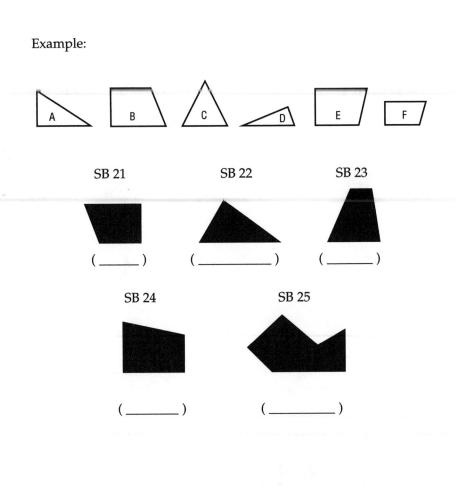

SB 21

(_____)

SB 22

(_____)

SB 23

(_____)

SB 24

(_____)

SB 25

(_____)

Following

The shapes on the left form a series. *Which of the letters of the shapes on the right continues the series?* Write the letter of the correct shape in the circle.

Example:

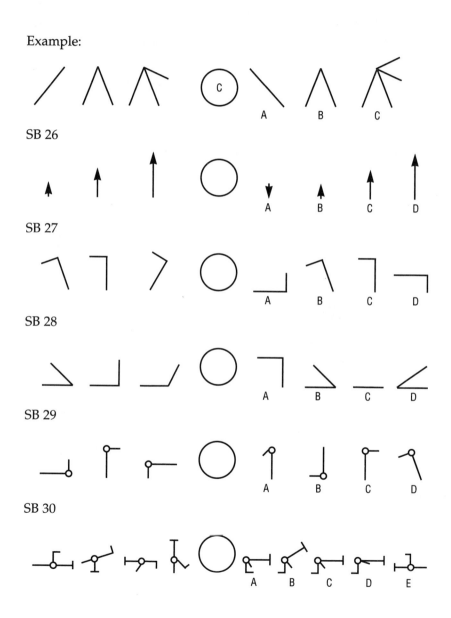

SB 26

SB 27

SB 28

SB 29

SB 30

Counting

The piles of blocks shown are solid. Any block without support is shown as such. Each diagram represents a pile of blocks, all of the same size and shape. Some blocks are lettered. Write a number beside each letter in the column on the right *to show how many blocks touch each lettered block*. A face, not just an edge, must touch. The first letter has been matched with a number as an example to show that block A touches three other blocks.

SB 31

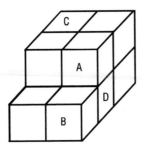

A	3	C	
B		D	

SB 32

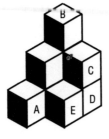

A		D	
B		E	
C			

SB33

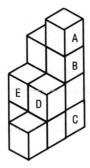

A		D	
B		E	
C			

SB 34

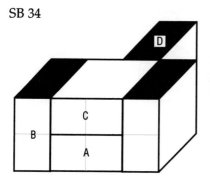

A		C	
B		D	

SB 35

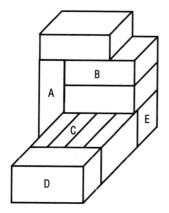

A		D	
B		E	
C			

93

Visualizing

Designs were drawn on some faces of these cubes. No design appears on the face of more than one cube. There are two blank faces on each cube. In each row some of the drawings are the same cube turned around. If a cube *can* be the same as another, assume it *is* the same. Write in the circle at the end of each row *the least number of different cubes represented in the row*. In the example, the second and third drawings are the same cube turned around.

Example:

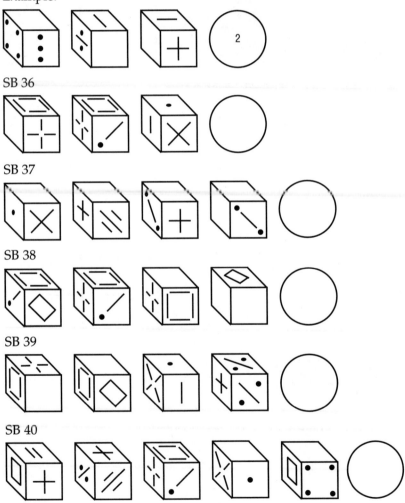

SB 36

SB 37

SB 38

SB 39

SB 40

Analogies

In each row, the first shape is related to the second shape in the same way that the third shape is related to the fourth. Underline *the figure on the right which should be the fourth shape.*

Example:

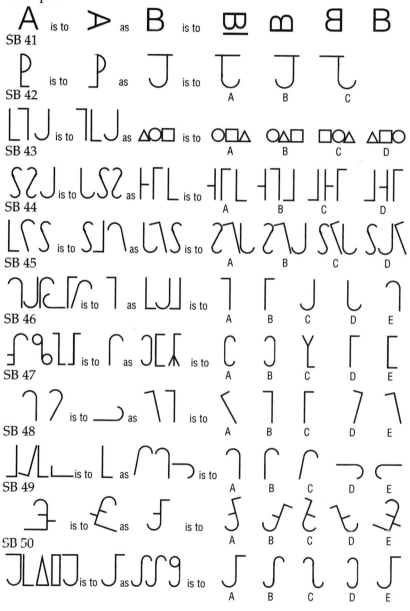

95

END OF TEST. CHECK YOUR WORK UNTIL TIME IS UP.
ANSWERS: p. 104.

ANSWERS TO VERBAL TEST A

VA 1. cup, saucer. VA 2. leader, follower (in the operation of sewing, the thread follows the needle). VA 3. rejoice, mourn (opposites). VA 4. window, view (a floor provides support and a window provides a view). VA 5. eyes, window (veils cover eyes as curtains cover windows). VA 6. divulge, reveal. VA 7. blessing, benediction. VA 8. intelligence, tidings ("intelligence" in the sense of "news"). VA 9. tale, story. VA 10. punish, chastise. VA 11. F (equally). VA 12. C (diminution). VA 13. L (write). VA 14. D (public). VA 15. E (remembrance). VA 16. H (unless). VA 17. G (new). VA 18. I (forgetful). VA 19. K (merit). VA 20. B (fame). VA 21. sea lion, whale (both mammals, the others are fish). VA 22. cloth and tinfoil (the others are made of compressed fibers). VA 23. arrow, dart (the others are used in the hand). VA 24. telephone, telegraph (the others *increase* the object). VA 25. love, fear (the others are detected by the senses). VA 26. dart. VA 27. form. VA 28. press. VA 29. fine. VA 30. fire. VA 31. deny, affirm. VA 32, veil, expose. VA 33. frank, secretive. VA 34. aggravate, improve. VA 35. primordial, ultimate. VA 36. is. VA 37. sometimes. VA 38. few. VA 39. transient. VA 40. ripe. VA 41. mercurial, phlegmatic (opposites). VA 42. object, demur (synonyms). VA 43. tenacious, irresolute (opposites). VA 44. literally, veritably (synonyms). VA 45. heap, hole (opposites). VA 46. selfish. VA 47. intrepid. VA 48. discord. VA 49. present. VA 50. yolk.

ANSWERS TO VERBAL TEST B

VB 1. father, boy. VB 2. face, eye. VB 3. center, perimeter. VB 4. cloud, coal (one is found high above earth, the other deep within it). VB 5. statue, marble (these are examples of form and content). VB 6. ray, beam. VB 7. collect, gather. VB 8. lazy, indolent. VB 9. divert, amuse. VB 10. bucolic, rustic. VB 11. D (none). VB 12. J (heaven). VB 13. E (individual). VB 14. F (unused). VB 15. H (suggests). VB 16. L (peers). VB 17. I (motive). VB 18. K (conduct). VB 19. B (distracted). VB 20. C (judgments). VB 21. needle, lance (the others have sharp *edges*). VB 22. disgust, fear (emotions; the others are virtues). VB 23. prosody, philosophy (aspects of literary culture; the others are sciences). VB 24. sieve, pickaxe (these separate things; the others fix them together). VB 25. receptionist, psychiatrist (main work is dealing with people; the others deal with things). VB 26. list. VB 27. tie. VB 28. match. VB 29. jam. VB 30. lash. VB 31. time. VB 32. within. VB 33. spheroid (ovoid means egg-shaped; a spheroid is the shape of the earth). VB 34. present. VB 35. partner. VB 36. shorten, extend. VB 37. intense, diffuse. VB 38. vex, pacify. VB 39. relate, disconnect. VB 40. intractable, obedient. VB 41. waist. VB 42. peer. VB 43. three (points have no dimensions, cubes three and lines one). VB 44. surgeon (probes and lancets are tools of surgeons as weapons are of soldiers). VB 45. navel (approximately center of body). VB 46. reliable, trustworthy (synonyms). VB 47. germane, apt (synonyms). VB 48. relegate, promote (opposites). VB 49. lucent, shining (synonyms). VB 50. lucubrate, grind (synonyms).

ANSWERS TO NUMBER TEST A

NA 1. 4. NA 2. –17. NA 3. 0.5 or $1/2$. NA 4. 2. NA 5. $1/128$. NA 6. 2 (divide the tail number by the sum of the numbers in the wings). NA 7. 11 (multiply together the wing numbers and add the tail number). NA 8. 48 (double the previous number). NA 9. 16 (each number is $2/3$ the previous number). NA 10. 33 (add to each successive number an amount double the difference between the previous pair of numbers). NA 11. 31 (add sixes). NA 12. 49 (the numbers are, successively, squares of 3, 4, 5, 6 and 7). NA 13. 9 (add upper squares; subtract lower squares). NA 14. 2 (multiply numbers in upper squares; subtract lower squares). NA 15. 11 (add numbers outside parentheses to give numbers inside). NA 16. 9 (multiply outer numbers to obtain inner number). NA 17. 112 (inner number is a quarter of the difference between outer numbers). NA 18. 168 (inner number is largest common factor of outer numbers). NA 19. 656 (inner number is twice the sum of outer numbers). NA 20. 2 (opposite numbers make 13). NA 21. 2 (the product of opposite numbers is 24). NA 22. 41 (each number is 6 less than the preceding one). NA 23. 19 (each number is 7 less than the preceding one). NA 24. 189 (each number is 27 less than the preceding one). NA 25. 17 (each number is half the preceding number after one is added to the preceding number). NA 26. 10 (each number is twice the preceding one, less two). NA 27. 20 (first column plus second gives third. First row plus second gives third). NA 28. 240 (in rows and columns, the first number and second are multiplied to give the third). NA 29. 5 (first two numbers minus the third gives the fourth). NA 30. 1 (the product of the first two numbers minus the third gives the fourth). NA 31. 3 (add the second and third numbers and subtract the first to give the fourth). NA 32. 5 (multiply the first two and add the third). NA 33. 3 (multiply the first two numbers and divide by the third). NA 34. 12 (in rows and columns, the first number multiplied by the second gives the third). NA 35. 2 (in rows and columns, the first number divided by the second gives the third). NA 36. 5 (the sum of numbers in triangles gives the answer). NA 37. 2 (the difference of numbers in triangles). NA 38. 12 (the product of numbers in triangle and square). NA 39. 1 (the number in the triangle is divided by the number in the circle). NA 40. 4 (add numbers in triangles and subtract numbers in inverted triangle). NA 41. 6 (multiply numbers in the triangle and the square, and divide by the number in the circle). NA 42. 4 (opposite numbers add up to 18). NA 43. 36 (opposite numbers multiplied give 36). NA 44. 9, 15 (the first number in each domino is two more and the second number is three more than in the domino before). NA 45. 8, 24 (the first number in the domino is two more and the second six more than in the domino before). NA 46. 22, 24 (the second number in each domino is twice that in the domino before, and the first number is 2 less than the second). NA 47. 4690, 4687 (the first number in each domino is the product of the numbers in the domino before; the second is three less). NA 48. 7, 343 (the first numbers in the domino are the natural series of odd numbers and the second are their cubes). NA 49. 6. NA 50. 126.

ANSWERS TO NUMBER TEST B

NB 1. 3. NB 2. –11. NB 3. 1.2. NB 4. 4. NB 5. 4/9. NB 6. 43 (multiply wing numbers, and add tail number). NB 7. 12 (multiply wing numbers, and subtract tail number). NB 8. 162 (each number is three times that before). NB 9. 81 (each number is three-quarters that before). NB 10. 31 (each number is twice that before, plus one). NB 11. 34 (each number is seven more than that before). NB 12. 121 (the series is: 7×7, 8×8, 9×9, 10×10, and 11×11). NB 13. 12 (add upper numbers and subtract lower numbers). NB 14. 3 (add upper numbers and subtract lower numbers). NB 15. 13 (the inner number is the sum of the outer numbers). NB 16. 10 (the inner number is the product of the outer numbers). NB 17. 131 (the inner number is one-third of the difference between the outer numbers). NB 18. 75 (the inner number is a quarter of the sum of the others). NB 19. 121 (the inner number is the largest number which is a factor of the outer numbers). NB 20. 8 (opposite numbers add up to 17). NB 21. 1 (the product of opposite numbers is 48). NB 22. 38 (each number is 7 less than that preceding). NB 23. 27 (each number is 8 less than that preceding). NB 24. 364 (each number is 26 less than that preceding). NB 25. 66 (each number is 13 less than that preceding). NB 26. 29 (each number is twice that before, plus three). NB 27. 19 (in columns and rows, the third number is the sum of the first two). NB 28. 180 (in columns and rows, the third number is the product of the first two). NB 29. 1 (add the first two numbers and subtract the third). NB 30. 11 (multiply the first two numbers and subtract the third). NB 31. 1 (add the first and third numbers and subtract the second). NB 32. 12 (multiply the first two numbers and add the third). NB 33. 16 (multiply the first two numbers and divide by the third). NB 34. 7 (the middle column numbers represent the sum of the other two). NB 35. 4 (divide numbers in the first column by corresponding numbers in the third and add one to obtain numbers in the middle column). NB 36. 7 (add numbers within the triangles). NB 37. 2 (the middle number is the difference between numbers in the triangles). NB 38. 18 (the middle number is the product of the others). NB 39. 7 (divide the first number by the third). NB 40. 3 (subtract the fourth number from the sum of the first and third). NB 41. 30 (the second number is the product of the others). NB 42. 13 (the sum of opposite numbers is 22). NB 43. 1 (the product of opposite numbers is 40). NB 44. 6, 10 (the first number in each domino is one more, and the second two more than in the domino before). NB 45. 5, 20 (the first number in each domino is one more than in the domino before, the second number is four times the first). NB 46. 2, 10 (the first number in each domino is one less, and the second one more than in the domino before). NB 47. 16, 4 (the second number in each domino is one less than in the domino before; the first number is the square of the second). NB 48. 15, 16 (the second number in each domino is twice the number in the domino before; the first number is one less than the second). NB 49. 60. NB 50. 42.

ANSWERS TO SPATIAL TEST A

SA 1. A, B. SA 2. A, D. SA 3. B, C. SA 4. A, D. SA 5. B, D. SA 6. A, C. SA 7. B, D. SA 8. A, D. SA 9. A, C. SA 10. A, C. SA 11. C. SA 12. A. SA 13. D. SA 14. C. SA 15. D. SA 16. A, D. SA 17. B, D. SA 18. B, D. SA 19. A, C. SA 20. B, D. SA 21. A. SA 22. D, F. SA 23. B. SA 24. E, F. SA 25. C, D. SA 26. B. SA 27. C. SA 28. D. SA 29. D. SA 30. A (the lines resemble clock hands). SA 31. C3, D3, E3. SA 32. A3, B3, C2, D2, E1. SA 33. A2, B2, C3, D3, E3. SA 34. A3, B5, C4, D3, E2. SA 35. A4, B4, C5, D4, E2. SA 36. one. SA 37. two (the first two represent the same cube). SA 38. two (the first and third represent the same cube). SA 39. two. (the first three represent the same cube). SA 40. three (the different designs *could* be the opposite three faces of two pairs and a single, therefore we assume that they *are*). SA 41. D. SA 42. A. SA 43. B (the feature face of the shape is turned from left to right and then put at the opposite end). SA 44. C (the second shape is the same as the odd one from the first set of shapes). SA 45. D. SA 46. C. SA 47. A. SA 48. D. SA 49. B. SA 50. C.

ANSWERS TO SPATIAL TEST B

SB 1. B, D. SB 2. C, E. SB 3. B, C. SB 4. A, C. SB 5. A, E. SB 6. A, C. SB 7. D, E. SB 8. A, E. SB 9. A, D. SB 10. A, D. SB 11. A. SB 12. C. SB 13. B. SB 14. D. SB 15. B. SB 16. A, D. SB 17. A, B. SB 18. B, D. SB 19. B, C. SB 20. A, C. SB 21. B. SB 22. A. SB 23. D, C. SB 24. E, F. SB 25. A, B, D. SB 26. D. SB 27. A. SB 28. C. SB 29. B. SB 30. C. SB 31. B2, C3, D4. SB 32. A1, B1, C2, D3, E2. SB 33. A1, B3, C3, D3, E3. SB 34. A4, B2, C4, D2. SB 35. A5, B3, C5, D4, E6. SB 36. two (the first two represent the same cube). SB 37. two (the first represents a cube different from the rest). SB 38. one. SB 39. two (the first two represent the same cube, the second two *can*). SB 40. three (the first and the last represent the same cube, the others *could* be a pair and a single). SB 41. C (the foot of the shape is turned from one side to the other). SB 42. B (the first and second units in the shape change places). SB 43. C (the last unit becomes the first and is transformed into its mirror image). SB 44. D (the first unit becomes second and is transformed into its mirror image; the last unit becomes first, and the second unit becomes last and its head turned around). SB 45. D (the shape most unlike the rest is transformed into its mirror image). SB 46. D (pick out the head of the shape whose head differs from its foot). SB 47. D (the series proceeds by units successively turning in a clockwise direction). SB 48. A (pick out the shape least resembling the others in virtue of laterality, or in terms of mirror images). SB 49. C (the first shape is transformed into the second shape by turning it in a clockwise direction through 45° after it has been transformed into a mirror image). SB 50. D (pick a shape which has a twin and turn its head from one side to the other).

CREATIVITY

If the concept "Intelligence" as a human personality factor is disputed, then the concept "Creativity" hardly exists at all. Creativity has a relatively thin background scientifically, but a suspiciously great fuss has been made about a surprisingly little body of actual experimental work. One feels the covert influence of the egalitarian environmentalists, the Procrustean Educational Levelers. Creativity is one of those compensatory ideas which flourish in this atmosphere. "Dim, yes," one hears the Procrusteans say, "but so creative!"

I shall try to consider creativity apart from its political undertones and overtones (or should I say egalitones?). Going by the evidence which is most convincing to me and least convincing to others—that is, personal experience—I feel that it *is* possible to separate people into classes by some criterion which could be reasonably called creativity. Some people are more adept at combining and recombining mental material into original forms. The difference appears to be in the field of hypothesis-making. If, as I believe, the process of solving problems is often a matter of trial and error, of adjusting and modifying conceptual frameworks until one with a relatively good fit is found, then "creatives" seem to me to be those who are more prolific at generating hypotheses. Their ability to judge the hypotheses when formed and to reject the inadequate would, in my intuitive view, be associated with pure intelligence. But their actual power and fruitfulness in producing sheer quantity of theories to be tested, though associated with intelligence, is not so closely associated.

The first studies in creativity were by Guilford and his associates in the U.S.A. in the early 1950s, and there are plenty of references to work on creativity over thirty years. Like other psychometric tests, creativity tests must be judged by whether they can be validated

105

statistically. Can the results be shown to have a relation to what we judge to be creativity in the world? W. H. Davies, for instance, picked out some Mensa members who, from information in the Mensa register, appeared to be "creative." He selected another group who, by their own register entries, appeared not to be so. By checking the scores of the two groups on the creativity tests he established a definite correlation. Creativity tests are not very suitable for self-marking and the tests which follow are for demonstration and amusement only. Only a very approximate indication of your "creativity" will emerge, and this only if you are very strict in marking yourself.

Instructions for First Creativity Test

In each square there are printed lines; use these as a basis for a separate, original drawing of something recognizable. Draw clearly but quickly. Do not bother with details. Do this first, then refer to the marking instructions printed on pages 112 and 113. Do not consult this before or you will be wasting your time. You have only five minutes to complete all the drawings.

Creativity (five-minute test)

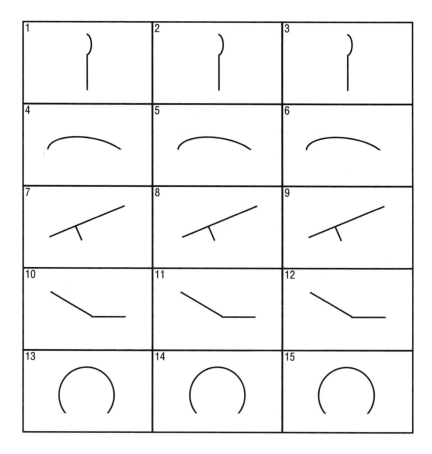

When you have finished turn to pages 112 and 113 to find out how to mark yourself.

TWO PERSONALITY TESTS

Here is another type of test. It has nothing to do with intelligence. There are no right or wrong answers to the questions.

Do the tests first and read about them afterward, otherwise your answers may be affected by what you read.

I shall call this first test Personality Factor No. 1. Try to answer quickly and spontaneously without giving the matter too much thought. It is your emotional reaction that is being checked, not your thought processes; so do not bother with doubts or possible illogicalities. Answer impulsively and quickly and pass on.

The key to the questions follows the key to the Creativity Test, which you'll find at the end of the Personality Factor No. 2.

Personality Factor 1

Circle your answer as A or B

1. Would you prefer to be a research scientist (A) or a member of Congress (B)?   A or B

2. Do you feel that many recognized professions or occupations which are accepted as honest do more harm to the country (A) than good (B)?   A or B

3. Which is more important in a literary critic, to be tolerant and encouraging (A) or carefully discriminating (B)?   A or B

4. If you had the choice of working as a receptionist (B) or at interesting work in an office of your own (A) which would you choose?   A or B

5. Should a doctor put his feelings aside in deciding about the treatment of his patients (A), or should his feelings be one of his main guides (B)?   A or B

6. Do you find it easy (B) or hard (A) to modify or adapt your behavior and everyday relationships according to the company you meet?   A or B

7. On vacation would you prefer to spend most of your time reading and on solitary walks (A) or would you prefer to spend most of your time meeting people (B)? A or B

8. Would you endure being a hermit easily (A) or with difficulty (B)? A or B

9. Would you prefer to marry a person who was (A) a thoughtful companion or (B) very sociable? A or B

10. Are most people probably (B) or doubtfully (A) worthy of real trust? A or B

11. Do you like (A) or dislike (B) organizing parties in general? A or B

12. Would you prefer being a traveling salesman (B) or a bookkeeper in an office (A)? A or B

13. Would you describe yourself as usually looking on the bright side of life (B) or being more cautious (A)? A or B

14. Would you prefer to be a high civil servant (A) or a member of the government (B)? A or B

15. Do you usually enjoy (B) or not enjoy (A) big noisy parties? A or B

16. Would you find it difficult (A) or easy (B) to make a public speech? A or B

17. In a dramatic production where would you be happier, working backstage (A) or as a leading actor (B)? A or B

18. Are you very ready (B) or more reserved (A) at making a suitable reply in most general conversation? A or B

19. Are you usually quick (B) or slow (A) at making new friends in a new situation? A or B

20. Would you describe yourself, in most of your activities, as being full of energy (B) or lacking in energy (A)? A or B

NOW GO ON TO THE NEXT TEST. DO NOT LOOK AT THE KEY YET.

Personality Factor 2

Again, you are asked to do the test first and check the result afterward. Peek if you want—but if you do, don't bother to check your result as it may be meaningless. Once again you should be in a decisive and uncontemplative frame of mind and go through the questions quickly and firmly, deciding how you feel about things rather than going into the logic or hesitating between one decision and another. The test should be completed in about 10 minutes, but it is of no great significance if you take more or less time.

1. As far as you know have you ever (A) or never (B) walked in your sleep?   A or B

2. Have you (A) or have you not (B) been away from work because of illness for a longer time than most people?   A or B

3. Do you (A) or do you not (B) have a tendency to feel confused if you are interrupted when working?   A or B

4. Are you (A) or are you not (B) fond of some hard exercise every day?   A or B

5. Remember the last time you began to learn a new skill: did you (B) or did you not (A) feel confident?   A or B

6. Have you (A) or have you not (B) felt strongly about everyday trivial irritations?   A or B

7. Have you ever (A) or have you never (B) worried for hours afterward about situations which felt humiliating to you?   A or B

8. Would many people (A) regard you as a sensitive person, or not (B)?   A or B

9. Do you (B) or do you not (A) usually get to sleep easily and sleep well?   A or B

10. Would many people (A) consider you to be shy, or not (B)?   A or B

11. Do you (A) or do you not (B) feel much put out or disturbed if someone you know fails to greet you?   A or B

12. Do you (A) or do you not (B) sometimes feel happy and sometimes feel sad without any real cause?   A or B

13. Do you (A) or do you not (B) find yourself day-dreaming often, when you should be working?   A or B

14. Can you (A) or can you not (B) remember having any nightmares in the last five years?   A or B

15. Have you (A) or have you not (B) a real fear of heights

or lifts or tunnels or going out of doors? A or B

16. Do you (B) or do you not (A) usually behave calmly and efficiently in an emergency? A or B

17. Do you (A) or do you not (B) believe yourself to be an emotional person in many of the situations of everyday life? A or B

18. Do you (A) or do you not (B) frequently worry about your health? A or B

19. Can you remember (A) or can you not remember (B) definitely annoying anyone in the last year? A or B

20. Do you (A) or do you not (B) perspire much without exercise? A or B

21. Within the last five years can you (A) or can you not (B) remember your mind going blank in the middle of doing a job? A or B

22. Within the last year have you met as many as three people that you have detected as being definitely unfriendly to you (A), or not (B)? A or B

23. Have you ever (A) or have you never (B) been short of breath without taking exercise? A or B

24. Are you generally tolerant of other people's odd little ways (B) or not (A)? A or B

25. Are there (A) or are there not (B) any normal everyday situations in which you feel definitely self-conscious? A or B

26. Do you often feel unhappy (A) or not (B)? A or B

27. Have you (A) or have you not (B) more than once suffered from diarrhea in the last two years? A or B

28. Are you usually self-confident (B) or not (A)? A or B

29. Have you (A) or have you not (B) any reason to believe that you cannot manage the situations of life as easily as most people? A or B

30. Do you (A) or do you not (B) use aspirin, codeine, sedatives, pep pills, sleeping pills or other drugs more than once a month nowadays? A or B

NOW COUNT YOUR A's AND B's. We will refer to them soon.

INSTRUCTIONS FOR MARKING
CREATIVITY TEST

Now comes the difficult part. Take one mark for each recognizable drawing, provided it does not fall into the same category as any other drawing on the same sheet. For instance, only one human face is allowed, and a second one gets no marks unless it is a detail in the drawing and not the whole subject. *You gain marks for the variety* (of ideas, scenes or things depicted) and *you are penalized for using the same idea twice.* If you are "creative" you will tend to variety naturally, even if you are not instructed.

There is no *right* answer to a creativity test; there are an infinite number of possible answers and they are all equally right provided they are novel and not copied, and provided they take into account all the features of the problem situation. In these problems you are asked to utilize the whole of the diagrams given. If any part of the diagram is not accommodated into your drawing, then you must go without the mark. It is, of course, best to get a friend to mark you, after getting him/her to read the instructions carefully.

There is still a good deal of argument about creativity tests and some people feel they are simply intelligence tests in disguise. R. W. Marsh in "A Statistical Re-Analysis of Getzels' and Jackson's Data," February 1964, said this: "rather than being almost independent of the general factor of intelligence, this (creativity) factor is the most constant and conspicuous ingredient . . . a conventional I.Q. is still the best single criterion for 'creative' potential. This may be improved on by the use of other tests as well." It was a study by Getzels and Jackson which first revived the examination of creativity. Getzels and Jackson found that of five schools examined, four showed that the top 20% for creativity performed as well as the top 20% for intelligence, although in each case they were in the bottom

80% as regards the opposite quality. The amount of excitement generated by this one not very conclusive study is interesting.

A more detailed and specialized system for "scoring" the test is given in the NORMS section of this book, following the concluding section on creativity.

KEY TO PERSONALITY FACTORS 1 AND 2

The first four tests correlate highly with general intelligence. It is obviously good to have an idea of this, but we have to recognize that there are many other important ways in which personality can be classified. Perhaps I should make it clear what I mean by personality. Everyone has different behavior patterns and these vary from time to time with mood changes, fits of temper, laughter, fear or joy. Behind this changing emotional pattern we are aware of deeper patterns and more permanent sets or tendencies which make it possible for us to classify people in a number of other ways.

Once the possibility of measuring things so intangible had been explored and found to be workable as regards intelligence, psychometricians began to look at many other personality factors to try to find out to what extent they would yield to the same rigorous statistical techniques. A whole world of expressions had grown up to describe human differences of this kind. Phlegmatic, cowardly, lazy, tough-minded, melancholic; hundreds of such terms exist. The psychometricians were confronted with a mass of different variables, all apparently widely understood and representing some real differences which (though difficult to define) seemed to have genuine predictive value.

In the hope of simplifying matters, which is always the job of a scientist, they worked on the assumption that there may be a relatively few independent parameters or dimensions of difference and that all the others derived from these. To check this they used their armory of statistical techniques to find out to what extent these factors related one to another. If there was a strong relation then it was assumed that there must be some common factor operating underneath. They found that they could be fitted into clusters or clumps which were interrelated.

The arguments about this are still going on. On the one hand

Professor Eysenck feels that, apart from intelligence, two principal dimensions account for most of the difference. On the other, Professor Raymond B. Cattell has, after a lifetime of work, come to the conclusion that there are sixteen relatively independent factors which make it possible to determine a complete description of the human personality. Apart from these, there is the Johnson's Temperament Analysis, Guilford's work and many others like them, each of which has its own rigorous statistical background but not too much in the way of common ground between them.

It is not a valid attack upon this kind of testing to say that the different ways of classifying the human personality are mutually inconsistent. When the human mind begins to look at phenomena it has to classify them first in order to deal with them at all. The laws which emerge are dependent on this original classification. Each set of laws is true in its own field or frame of reference. Eventually, scientists agree on the most useful way of classifying phenomena and from that point forward the science usually grows and flourishes. But in the early, difficult days of a science many different classification methods are tried out before the most effective and predictive is discovered. The "truth" of any of them is like the truth of any epistemological law—this, that it is part of the science of knowledge. This means simply that the answers we get depend on the questions we ask. Some questions turn out to be more useful than others, some are the damn silly questions which infallibly attract damn silly answers.

In trying to measure his own qualities mankind is examining the most complicated thing he knows in the universe, and it is not surprising that science in this field has not made the progress that it has in some others.

As I have said, the proper utilization and the happiness of people in the developed world today depends on their fitting precisely and well into a thousand different and highly specified roles. We can fit them by a hit-and-miss, trial-and-error method if we choose, but if we are wise we will not neglect even these early discoveries of psychometric science to help us to do the job wisely, sanely and without prejudice.

In this part of the book I have chosen only two exemplary parameters of personality measurement. These two factors are independent of intelligence. The two factors concerned are extroversion–introversion (Personality Factor 1) and emotional stability (Personality Factor 2).

Personality Factor 1 (Extroverts and Introverts)

The extrovert and introvert represent the extremes and most people are somewhere in between. People vary from time to time and will be more extroverted on some occasions and less on others. But usually they tend to remain about the same, with, over a long term, a slight trend towards extroversion.

The extrovert is the outward-looking, socially friendly and uninhibited type of person. He/she enjoys company, feels at ease in a large circle and tends to form a large number of relatively shallow relationships. Confident, assertive and friendly, we can represent this extreme type as a boisterous, talkative and friendly commercial traveler who is very much at home in a bar or at the club. The extreme introvert might be a professor or accountant, one who is much more at home in his study or taking long solitary walks with a pipe, a stick and a dog. Introverts tend to form one or a few profound attachments, enjoy books, chess and thought. They are the type who like to keep themselves *to* themselves and slightly disapprove of neighbors who are "always in and out of one another's houses." Neither type of personality is good or bad, although it is probably preferable to be somewhere in between. Those who are extremely extroverted, according to Eysenck, have a higher probability of being criminals if they also lack emotional stability; of course, many people with very high extroversion scores and low scores on emotional stability are perfectly honest and respectable. Again, I speak only of a tendency and not of an invariable relation.

The more A's you got the more introverted you are. 15 or so would make you definitely introverted, and 20 very much so. 15 B's make you an extrovert, and 20 a bouncing extrovert like me (and jolly good luck to you too).

116

Personality Factor 2 (Emotional Stability)

This test has been called a test of neuroticism, but it might be more tactful to say it is a test of stability against emotional sensitivity. The answers you give decide whether you are emotionally sensitive or impervious. *Those with 20 or so B's are very imperturbable,* people who never seem to get upset, who are equable and balanced and who probably go though life without the ups and downs of the more sensitive type of person. *If you have a score of more than 20 A's you are emotional and suggestible,* and probably feel the mental strains of life more than most, needing plenty of rest and the sort of work, friendships and hobbies that can make a stable background for you. On the other hand, those with 22 or so B's might ask themselves whether they are not a bit too phlegmatic and might try to arrange life so as to present some challenge to their placidity or even unresponsiveness.

Professor Eysenck shows how these two factors neatly account for the full range of Aristotle's character types. Choleric is extroverted and unstable, melancholic is introverted and unstable, phlegmatic is introverted and stable, and sanguine is extroverted and stable.

CONCLUSION TO CREATIVITY

Now that you have finished this part of the book you can classify yourself "dim—melancholic, bright—phlegmatic, dull—sanguine, brilliant—choleric" or whatever, you may be a little wiser about yourself and a little better able to adjust your behavior to all those other thick introverts, dim extroverts and melancholic geniuses around you. Even if you can't do this I hope you have got some idea about intelligence and personality testing and why, in the modern world, it is more important than it was. Perhaps we cannot at the moment claim very much for it. It is a science in its infancy; the need for it is not yet fully understood. We do not spend enough money, and the progress made in it is inadequate.

I sometimes wonder about the whole process of education. We enter all our children from birth in an agonizing educational rat race which occupies them all though their childhood and much of their youth (often, I fear, because of the competitive scrambling for academic qualifications, to the exclusion of the real process of education). Is this really the best way? Are the psychometrics right when they hint that it may be possible to know much about the results of this process before we start it; to give each child the educational and emotional training best suited for him or her and for society too? We do not have sufficient information on this today, but there can hardly be a subject of greater importance. Yet the money spent on psychological research of this type is pitifully small. If there is a more important science than that of judging and using humans justly, fairly and in accordance with their powers, I do not know what it is. But going by the money spent in this country, nothing is more important than getting faster airplanes; so the human contents of the country (and the airplanes) will have to sort themselves out in the future, as in the past, by the well-tried methods of social class, privilege, racial discrimination, influence, the academic old-grad network and all the other traditional, inefficient and unfair methods.

"Should our children be 'condemned' from an early stage?" "Everyone should have an equal chance." These are the reactions I shall get, but the sad and unavoidable fact is that everyone has *not* got an equal chance of becoming a professor, a ballet dancer or a champion runner—so why should we let so many youngsters break their hearts trying for something they can never get, when we have or could have the means to let them know in advance what the chances are?

It would not be necessary to "condemn" anyone to the lower academic streams if they were really determined to try for the higher ones. The system should be permeable. Openings should be left for some to defy the diagnosis. But most people would rather *know* what the chances are before they start anything, and the argument for not wanting to know and finding out the hard way is very thin and feeble. It is no denial of human freedom to give people the information on which to make their decisions. It is a denial of human freedom to deny people the knowledge which may guide them to make the right decisions in seeking happiness, adjustment and the best and most useful place to serve mankind with the particular qualities they were born with or have been inclined to develop. "To each according to his needs, from each according to his ability." The second is as important as the first. It is not the rights and privileges of the intelligent I am concerned with. They can, I fear, look after themselves all too well in these respects. I am worried about such people's duties, responsibilities and contributions in a world which needs more and more intelligent people as it develops.

NORMS:

Verbal Test A			Verbal Test B	
Marks	*Quotients*		*Marks*	*Quotients*
0 – 5	85 – 95		0 – 5	85 – 95
6 – 12	96 – 105		6 – 10	96 – 105
13 – 18	106 – 112		11 – 15	106 – 112
19 – 25	113 – 118		16 – 20	113 – 118
26 – 30	119 – 122		21 – 25	119 – 122
31 – 35	123 – 128		26 – 30	123 – 128
36 – 40	129 – 131		31 – 35	129 – 131
41 – 45	132 – 137		36 – 38	132 – 137
46 – 49	138 – 140+		39 – 45	138 – 140+

A mark of about 40 on this test might indicate that a person would stand a good chance of obtaining Mensa membership after more thorough testing.

A mark of about 35 on this test might indicate that a person would stand a good chance of obtaining Mensa membership after more thorough testing.

Number Test A

Marks	Quotients
0 – 5	85 – 92
6 – 10	93 – 97
11 – 15	98 – 102
16 – 20	103 – 107
21 – 25	108 – 112
26 – 30	113 – 117
31 – 35	118 – 122
36 – 40	123 – 127
41 – 45	128 – 132
46 – 50	133 – 137+

Number Test B

Marks	Quotients
0 – 5	85 – 97
6 – 10	98 – 102
11 – 15	103 – 107
16 – 20	108 – 112
21 – 25	113 – 117
26 – 30	118 – 122
31 – 35	123 – 127
36 – 40	128 – 132
41 – 45	133 – 137
46 – 50	138 – 140+

Spatial Tests A and B

Marks	Quotients
0 – 5	85 – 95
6 – 10	96 – 105
11 – 15	106 – 110
16 – 20	111 – 114
21 – 25	115 – 119
26 – 30	120 – 124
31 – 35	125 – 129
36 – 40	130 – 134
41 – 45	135 – 138
46 – 50	139 – 140+

ODIOUS COMPARISONS:
HOW TO INTERPRET YOUR SCORE

The intelligence test consists of a battery of three tests. These test special abilities, which are a guide to general ability and are the factors we are trying to measure.

For each question you answer correctly you get one mark. There is no penalty for wrong answers.

The number of marks is called the "raw score." From the raw score we can read off the "quotient."

The Intelligence Quotient or I.Q. is a confusing technical expression which should never have become popular. Strictly it applies to children and only by extrapolation to adults. It is the mental age multiplied by 100 divided by the actual age. If a child of 10 can perform as well as the average child of 15, its I.Q. is $\frac{15 \times 100}{10} = 150$.

The average I.Q. is (naturally, therefore) 100.

Unfortunately the different psychologists produce different results from Binet's primitive scheme, so that an I.Q. score means different things on different tests according to the standard deviation.

A preferable way of judging I.Q. is by percentile rating. Your percentile rating is that percentage of the general population (upon whom the test was standardized) which your performance equals or excels. If you score 40 on Verbal Test A your I.Q. is 131 and you fall in the 98th percentile; that is, you would score better than or equal to 98% of people in general.

The verbal scores have a heavier "g" loading, and we represent that by multiplying them by 3.

Add the total of the four Number and Spatial Test quotients to 3 times the total of the two Verbal Tests quotient and divide by 10. This gives an estimate of I.Q.

HERE'S HOW YOU CAN FIND OUT YOUR I.Q. FROM YOUR SCORE:

	Score		*Quotient*
Number A			
Number B			
Spatial A			
Spatial B			
			_____
			TOTAL

	Score		*Quotient*
Verbal A			
Verbal B			
			_____
			TOTAL

Multiply Verbal total by 3 =

Add Number/Spatial total =

TOTAL

I.Q.=Final total ÷ 10

YOUR I.Q.

YOUR CREATIVITY, JUDGED BY YOUR RESULTS ON THE 5-MINUTE CREATIVITY TEST

Number of complete, original, unrepetitive drawings:

1	UNCREATIVE
2	
3	
4	
5	
6	
7/8	AVERAGE
9	
10	
11	
12	
13	
14	
15	VERY CREATIVE

YOUR INTROVERSION/EXTROVERSION, JUDGED BY YOUR RESULTS ON THE PERSONALITY FACTOR TEST 1

No. of A's	*Character*
20	EXTREMELY INTROVERTED
19	VERY INTROVERTED
18	QUITE INTROVERTED
16/17	SOMEWHAT INTROVERTED
14/15	SLIGHTLY INTROVERTED
12/13	A SHADE INTROVERTED
9/10/11	AVERAGE
7/8	A SHADE EXTROVERTED
5/6	SLIGHTLY EXTROVERTED
3/4	SOMEWHAT EXTROVERTED
2	QUITE EXTROVERTED
1	VERY EXTROVERTED
0	EXTREMELY EXTROVERTED

YOUR STABILITY, JUDGED BY YOUR RESULTS ON THE PERSONALITY FACTOR TEST 2

No. of B's	Character
29/30	UNSHAKABLE
28/27	IMPERTURBABLE
26/25	UNFLAPPABLE
24/23	CALM
22/21	BALANCED
20/19/18	STEADY
17/16/15/14	AVERAGE
13/12/11	SYMPATHETIC
10/9	SUGGESTIBLE
8/7	EMOTIONAL
6/5	SENSITIVE
4/3	OVERSENSITIVE
2/1	NERVOUS
0	NEUROTIC

How did you do?   You *did!*   No!

Good-bye you intelligent, creative, balanced ambivert thing, you! If you are good-looking, charming and a go-getter too, how you *will* be hated. . . .